MACMILLAN MASTER GUIDES

General Editor: James ⬚

Published:

JANE AUSTEN: **PRIDE AND** ⬚ ⬚ stamped below.
   EMMA Norman Page
   MANSFIELD PARK Rich⬚
ROBERT BOLT: **A MAN FOR ALL SEASO**⬚
EMILY BRONTË: **WUTHERING HEIGHTS** Hil⬚
GEOFFREY CHAUCER: **THE PROLOGUE TO**
   Nigel Thomas and Ric⬚
   THE MILLER'S TALE Mic⬚
CHARLES DICKENS: **BLEAK HOUSE** Dennis Butts
   GREAT EXPECTATIONS Dennis Butts
   HARD TIMES Norman Page
GEORGE ELIOT: **MIDDLEMARCH** Graham Handley
   SILAS MARNER Graham Handley
E. M. FORSTER: **A PASSAGE TO INDIA** Hilda D. Spear
THE METAPHYSICAL POETS Joan van Emden
WILLIAM GOLDING: **LORD OF THE FLIES** Raymond Wilson
OLIVER GOLDSMITH: **SHE STOOPS TO CONQUER** Paul Ranger
THOMAS HARDY: **FAR FROM THE MADDING CROWD** Colin Temblett-Wood
   TESS OF THE D'URBERVILLES James Gibson
CHRISTOPHER MARLOWE: **DOCTOR FAUSTUS** David A. Male
ARTHUR MILLER: **THE CRUCIBLE** Leonard Smith
GEORGE ORWELL: **ANIMAL FARM** Jean Armstrong
WILLIAM SHAKESPEARE: **MACBETH** David Elloway
   A MIDSUMMER NIGHT'S DREAM Kenneth Pickering
   ROMEO AND JULIET Helen Morris
   THE WINTER'S TALE Diana Devlin
   HENRY IV PART I Helen Morris
GEORGE BERNARD SHAW: **ST JOAN** Leonée Ormond
RICHARD SHERIDAN: **THE RIVALS** Jeremy Rowe
   THE SCHOOL FOR SCANDAL Paul Ranger

Forthcoming:
SAMUEL BECKETT: **WAITING FOR GODOT** J. Birkett
WILLIAM BLAKE: **SONGS OF INNOCENCE AND SONGS OF EXPERIENCE**
   A. Tomlinson
GEORGE ELIOT: **THE MILL ON THE FLOSS** H. Wheeler
T. S. ELIOT: **MURDER IN THE CATHEDRAL** P. Lapworth
HENRY FIELDING: **JOSEPH ANDREWS** T. Johnson
E. M. FORSTER: **HOWARD'S END** I. Milligan
WILLIAM GOLDING: **THE SPIRE** R. Sumner
THOMAS HARDY: **THE MAYOR OF CASTERBRIDGE** R. Evans
SELECTED POEMS OF GERALD MANLEY HOPKINS
PHILIP LARKIN: **THE WHITSUN WEDDING AND THE LESS DECEIVED**
   A. Swarbrick
D. H. LAWRENCE: **SONS AND LOVERS** R. Draper
HARPER LEE: **TO KILL A MOCKINGBIRD** Jean Armstrong
THOMAS MIDDLETON: **THE CHANGELING** A. Bromham
ARTHUR MILLER: **DEATH OF A SALESMAN** P. Spalding
WILLIAM SHAKESPEARE: **HAMLET** J. Brooks
   HENRY V P. Davison
   KING LEAR F. Casey
   JULIUS CAESAR David Elloway
   MEASURE FOR MEASURE M. Lilly
   OTHELLO Christopher Beddows
   RICHARD II C. Barber
   TWELFTH NIGHT Edward Leeson
   THE TEMPEST Kenneth Pickering
TWO PLAYS OF JOHN WEBSTER David A. Male

Also published by Macmillan

MASTERING ENGLISH LITERATURE R. Gill
MASTERING ENGLISH LANGUAGE S. H. Burton
MASTERING ENGLISH GRAMMAR S. H. Burton

WORK OUT SERIES

WORK OUT ENGLISH LANGUAGE ('O' level and GCSE) S. H. Burton
WORK OUT ENGLISH LITERATURE ('A' level) S. H. Burton

MACMILLAN MASTER GUIDES
THE CRUCIBLE
BY ARTHUR MILLER

LEONARD SMITH

MACMILLAN

First published 1986 by
THE MACMILLAN PRESS LTD
Houndmills, Basingstoke, Hampshire RG21 2XS
and London
Companies and representatives
throughout the world

ISBN 0–333–39772–X

A catalogue record for this book is available
from the British Library.

Printed in China

Reprinted 1993

CONTENTS

GENERAL EDITOR'S PREFACE

The aim of the Macmillan Master Guides is to help you to appreciate the book you are studying by providing information about it and by suggesting ways of reading and thinking about it which will lead to a fuller understanding. The section on the writer's life and background has been designed to illustrate those aspects of the writer's life which have influenced the work, and to place it in its personal and literary context. The summaries and critical commentary are of special importance in that each brief summary of the action is followed by an examination of the significant critical points. The space which might have been given to repetitive explanatory notes has been devoted to a detailed analysis of the kind of passage which might confront you in an examination. Literary criticism is concerned with both the broader aspects of the work being studied and with its detail. The ideas which meet us in reading a great work of literature, and their relevance to us today, are an essential part of our study, and our Guides look at the thought of their subject in some detail. But just as essential is the craft with which the writer has constructed his work of art, and this is considered under several technical headings – characterisation, language, style and stagecraft.

The authors of these Guides are all teachers and writers of wide experience, and they have chosen to write about books they admire and know well in the belief that they can communicate their admiration to you. But you yourself must read and know intimately the book you are studying. No one can do that for you. You should see this book as a lamppost. Use it to shed light, not to lean against. If you know your text and know what it is saying about life, and how it says it, then you will enjoy it, and there is no better way of passing an examination in literature.

JAMES GIBSON

ACKNOWLEDGEMENTS

The author and publishers wish to thank Elaine Greene Ltd. on behalf of Arthur Miller for kindly giving permission to use extracts from *The Crucible* in *Collected Plays by Arthur Miller*, published by Secker & Warburg Ltd. Copyright © 1952, 1953 by Arthur Miller.

Every effort has been made to trace all the copyright holders but if any have been inadvertently overlooked the publishers will be pleased to make the necessary arrangement at the first opportunity.

Cover illustration: The Golden Age by Benjamin West © Tate Gallery Publications.

1 INTRODUCTION

The Crucible in its printed form, which Arthur Miller says in the early editions 'is designed for the reading public only', contains long comments by Miller himself on the background to the play and on the characters. These comments are interspersed among the dialogue in Act one and form no part of the play itself. The examination boards recommend that you should study this 'reading edition' because Miller's own comments are extremely pertinent.

However, although you are recommended to use the 'reading edition' for your study, you should never forget that *The Crucible* is a work of art designed to be performed on a stage. Only in performance can it have its full dramatic effect. If you are not lucky enough to see a performance, you must imagine how it would appear on the stage. The dramatic impact of the play depends not only on the words spoken by the actors, but also on the effects of costumes, stage properties, sounds on and off stage, lighting, and other theatrical devices, including the reactions of the audience.

So don't study *The Crucible* as you would a novel, short story or poem. You must read not only the words spoken by the characters, but also imagine how they would be delivered on the stage; you must read all the stage directions carefully, and imagine what effect they would have, not only the visual effects of costumes, props, changes of scene and the use of lighting, but also the sounds. Arthur Miller, you will find, is a master at using off-stage sounds to great effect.

The dialogue and the stage directions in the 'reading edition' are exactly the same as in the acting edition. The 'Summary and Critical Commentary' in Section 3 of this book concentrates on the dialogue and stage directions, that is the play itself. Miller's own comments are used to elucidate certain points in Section 4, 'The Historical Sources of the Play', and in Section 5, 'Themes'.

When you feel you have a good understanding of the play, go back and read it through, missing out Arthur Miller's comments. If you cannot organise a performance, try to arrange a dramatic reading of the play, taking parts and putting as much expression into the voices as possible. Although the play needs a production in a theatre to achieve its full effect, the dialogue itself is so powerful that a good dramatic reading can be most moving.

2 ARTHUR MILLER AND THE BACKGROUND TO THE PLAY

2.1 EARLY LIFE

Arthur Miller was born in New York City on 17 October 1915, the second of three children. His father was a fairly successful manufacturer of ladies' coats, and his mother was a schoolteacher. They were a Jewish family and observed Jewish holidays and customs, but they were not strictly Orthodox; the younger generation regarded themselves as American rather than Jewish. In 1929 the Millers moved out to Brooklyn, which was then a semi-rural suburb, and where many of their relatives and other Jewish families had established themselves.

Arthur Miller, in an article he wrote for the magazine *Holiday* in 1955, indicates that he had a comfortable childhood. At school he was more distinguished at football and athletics than he was as a scholar, so when he graduated from high school in 1932 his academic record was not good enough to obtain a place at university.

After this disappointment he went to work in his father's business, an experience he thoroughly disliked. But when he tried to strike out on his own, he became aware at first hand of the unemployment caused by the Great Depression which had followed the Wall Street crash of 1929: there were not many jobs around, and even less for a Jewish young man. For a year he worked in a car-parts warehouse in Manhattan, and Miller has said that during this year he read more than he had at any time in his life. A key book was the nineteenth-century Russian writer Fyodor Dostoyevsky's *Brothers Karamazov* which he later called 'the great book of wonder' with 'its most colourful, breathtaking, wonderful pages'. Miller's adolescent years had not proved to be as smooth as his childhood days had been. He later said of this time that he began to see 'how things connected, how the native personality of man was changed by his world, and the harder question, how he could in turn change his world'. The Depression, which ruined so many businesses, including that of Miller's father, and which caused so many people to suffer unemployment and hardship, had a lasting effect on Miller's thinking. One of his biographers, Neil Carson, calls it 'the most formative crisis in Miller's life'. Even one of Miller's latest plays, *The American Clock* (1982), opens with these words: 'There have been only two American disasters that were truly national. . .Only the Civil War and the Great Depression touched nearly everyone wherever they lived and whatever their social class. Personally, I believe that deep down we are still afraid that suddenly, without warning, it may all fall apart again.'

2.2 UNIVERSITY AND FIRST PLAYS

About twenty years later Miller recalled his experience of working in the warehouse when writing *A Memory of Two Mondays* (1955), a play in which most of the characters are trapped in a monotonous routine. One character, Bert, like Miller himself, had felt the power of literature and saves enough money to go off to college. Miller, wanting to be a writer, reapplied in 1934 to the University of Michigan to study journalism and was given a place on condition that he completed his first year successfully.

Life at university opened out whole new areas of life for him. With the rise of Fascism in Europe and the overthrow of democracy in Spain during the Spanish Civil War (1936–9), the campus was alive with political discussion and activity, and Miller found himself leaning increasingly towards socialist ideas: like many idealistic young people of that time, he believed in change and progress in society, and thought that he could help to bring about that change. The Depression had shown the inhumanity of the 'American system'.

But college life was not only politics. He did part-time jobs, one as a night editor of a newspaper. And during his second year, although he had been to a theatre only once or twice in his life, he wrote a play, *Honors at Dawn*, and submitted it for the university's Hopwood Drama Award. To his surprise, he won the first prize of $250. His career as a playwright had begun.

Encouraged by his success, Miller enrolled on a play-writing course, and in the following year, 1937, he again won the Drama Award with *No Villain*. He then revised this second play, renamed it *They Too Arise*, and won the Theater Guild Bureau of New Plays Award of $1250, and had the play produced in Ann Arbor and Detroit.

These plays have never been published, but they showed Miller that he could write. They also gave him the experience of investigating in dramatic form some of the themes, such as social responsibility and individual conscience and respect, that he was to explore in his mature plays.

2.3 THE DEPRESSION

After his more sheltered and purposeful life as a student, when Miller left university in 1938 with a BA degree, he found himself once again unemployed. The Depression had caught up with him again. But he now knew what he wanted to do with his life – to write plays, and not just plays for entertainment, but drama which 'ought to help us to know more', and to 'open up new relationships between man and men, and between men and Man'. He was influenced here by the work of the Group Theatre, a team of mainly Left-wing artists who believed that the theatre had a social role to play. Miller himself said of the Group, whose productions he used to watch from 55¢ seats in the balcony: 'Here was the promise of prophetic theatre which suggested to my mind the Greek situation when religion and belief were the heart of drama.' By 'prophetic' Miller explained that he meant 'a play which is meant to become part of the lives of its audience – a play seriously meant for people of common sense, and relevant to both their domestic lives and their daily work, but an experience which widens their awareness of connection – the filaments to the past and the future which lie concealed in "life".'

In 1938 he joined the Federal Theatre Project which had been set up to give work to unemployed actors, technicians and writers, and with a friend he wrote a satirical sketch, *Listen My Children*, about collecting unemployment relief. But next year the project was wound up when Congress refused to sponsor it because of alleged communist influence. This was Miller's first brush with the recently formed House Committee on Un-American Activities, which was later to have a major impact on his life as a dramatist.

At this time Miller married Mary Slattery, whom he had met at university. She worked in a publishing house, and he did various odd jobs, including truck driving, to support them while he tried to make his name as a dramatist. He wrote several plays, but none of them satisfied him. To make a little money, he also wrote radio scripts, although he despised the medium. But in one of these plays, *The Pussycat and the Expert Plumber Who Was a Man*, he explored, satirically, some important themes. Tom, the cat, says: 'The one thing a man fears most next to death is the loss of his good name', and 'Some men. . .are so proud of their usefulness that they don't need the respect of their neighbours and so they aren't afraid to speak the truth.' One of his stage plays, *The Man Who Had All the Luck*, was published and accepted for production in 1944, but it closed after only four performances. It had been noticed, however, by the producer Harold Clurman, who had been associated with the Group Theatre, and who was to be one of the producers of Miller's first Broadway success.

2.4 WARTIME

Miller was unable to join any of the armed forces during the Second World War because of an old football injury, but he started working on a film to be called *The Story of G.I. Joe*. He visited camps and battle schools, interviewing dozens of soldiers, collecting background material for the film. He then used this experience of talking to soldiers in a book of reportage called *Situation Normal*, published in 1944, and bringing Miller his first notices in national newspapers. In 1945 he published a novel, *Focus*, whose main character, although not Jewish, suffered from Anti-Semitism because he looked like a Jew when he had to wear glasses. But although both these books widened his experience of writing, and brought him favourable reviews, neither provided him with the breakthrough he needed. He knew his true talent was for stage drama, if only he could find his way through to the right theme, and the right form and style for expressing it.

2.5 FIRST SUCCESS

The theme for his first success came to him quite by chance; but, as the French chemist and microbiologist Louis Pasteur (1822–95) said, 'Chance favours the prepared mind'. A relative told him about a girl who had denounced her father when she found out that he had been knowingly supplying defective parts for military aircraft during the war, causing the death of many airmen. Miller immediately saw the possibility for a drama involving conflict in the family, but revealing a man's responsibilities beyond his front gate. Through being brought to realise his place in a wider community, a man is brought to 'know himself'.

It took Miller two years to write *All My Sons*; it opened on 29 January 1947 and ran for 328 performances. Miller said that his first success was 'somewhat like pushing against a door which is suddenly opened from the other side...It suddenly seemed that the audience was a mass of blood relations and I sensed a warmth in the world that had not been there before...I tasted that power which is reserved, I imagine, for playwrights, which is to know that by one's invention a mass of strangers had been publicly transfixed.'

2.6 *DEATH OF A SALESMAN*

With the money he earned from *All My Sons*, Miller bought a house in Brooklyn and a farm in Roxbury, Connecticut, where he built a cabin in the grounds where he could write. By this time he had a son and a daughter.

In this cabin he started working on a play about some people in an industrial town during the Depression. But the drama wouldn't come together. Suddenly, one evening, he found his mind full of images about a salesman he had known during the short period he had worked in his father's clothing business. He worked feverishly through the night, and by morning about two-thirds of a play was finished in first draft. He called it *The Inside of His Head* because the impression he wanted to give was that all the action was taking place in the salesman's head – his dreams, memories and ambitions for his sons. Once again the impulse for the dramatic tension was conflict in the family, but with wider implications.

It took Miller only three months to complete the play. He realised later that the seed had been sown much earlier with a play he had started as a student. Although it made no progress then, the theme of the salesman as the symbol of the false 'drive' and 'success' in the American way of life, had been developing in his subconscious all those years and now flowered into consciousness.

When it opened on Broadway in 1949, as *Death of a Salesman*, it ran for 742 performances. It won many drama awards, and was performed all over the world. After years of struggle, Miller had become an internationally acclaimed playwright.

2.7 THE COMMITTEE ON UN-AMERICAN ACTIVITIES

The feeling of euphoria was short-lived. As Miller himself said: 'If the reception of *All My Sons* and *Death of a Salesman* had made the world a friendly place for me, events of the early fifties quickly turned that warmth into an illusion.' The Committee on Un-American Activities caught up with him again.

Although disbanded during the war, when Russia was an ally of the USA and Britain in the fight against Hitler's Germany, the House Committee on Un-American Activities was revived in 1945 to investigate the infiltration of communists into American institutions. In its search for 'enemies of the state' the Committee, under its zealous chairman Senator Joseph McCarthy, could call any witness it liked. Since they were not technically accused of anything, the witnesses were not protected by any of the usual legal procedures, and could not call their counsel to defend them. Witnesses were not accused of doing anything illegal, but of being under suspicion of harbouring un-American beliefs and thoughts. Hearsay, prejudice and allegation assumed the authority of legal proof, and the widest publicity was given to 'unfriendly' witnesses. Those who pleaded the First or Fifth Amendment of the Constitution not to answer any question, were generally assumed to be guilty. In the atmosphere of mass hysteria that was built up, many witnesses, although completely innocent of any crime, found themselves ostracised by their friends, dismissed from their jobs, and even under physical threat from some over-zealous 'patriots'. The fear engendered caused many suicides.

Although *The Crucible* is not 'about' the activities of the Un-American Activities Committee, there is no doubt, as Miller said himself, that '"what was in the air" provided the actual locus of the tale'. There is no better analysis of its influence on the play than what Miller himself wrote in the Introduction to the *Collected Plays*:

> It was not only the rise of 'McCarthyism' that moved me, but something which seemed much more weird and mysterious. It was the fact that a political, objective, knowledgeable campaign from the far Right was capable of creating not only a terror, but a new subjective reality, a veritable mystique which was gradually assuming even a holy resonance. The wonder of it all struck me that so practical and picayune a cause, carried forward by such manifestly ridiculous men, should be capable of paralysing thought itself, and worse, causing to billow up such persuasive clouds of 'mysterious' feelings within people. It was as though the whole country had been born anew, without a memory even of certain elemental decencies which a year or two earlier no one would have imagined could be altered, let alone forgotten. Astounded, I watched men pass me by without a nod whom I had known rather well for years; and, again, the astonishment was produced by my knowledge, which I could not give up, that the terror in these people was being knowingly planned and consciously engineered, and yet that all they knew was terror. That so interior and subjective an emotion could have been so manifestly created from without was a marvel to me. It underlies every word in *The Crucible*. . .Above all, above all horrors, I saw accepted the notion that conscience was no longer a private matter but one of state administration. I saw men handing conscience to other men and thanking other men for the opportunity of doing so.

2.8 MILLER SUBPOENAED

The Crucible opened in New York on 22 January 1953 and ran for 197 performances. It won the Antoinette Perry and the Donaldson Prizes as the most distinguished American drama of the year, but many people saw the play as an attack on the Un-American Activities Committee, and the conservative first-night audience received it coldly. The world was not now such a friendly place for Miller, and it was rapidly to become openly hostile.

In September 1955 two new plays, *A View from the Bridge* and *A Memory of Two Mondays* opened in New York and had generally unfavourable reviews, although the weakness was chiefly in faulty acting and production. But this theatrical failure (although the plays ran for 147 performances) was nothing compared with the political and personal dramas that were developing around Miller.

In 1955 he had started working on a film which would record the work of the Youth Board of New York City in its attempt to rehabilitate members of the violent street gangs. Various ex-servicemen's organisations protested about public money being spent to supplement the work of a 'known communist', and although Miller denied that he was a communist, the Youth Board caved in under the smear campaign and dropped the project.

In 1956 when Miller applied for a passport to visit Brussels for a production of *The Crucible*, he was subpoenaed to appear before the Committee as a witness, ostensibly to help them with their investigations into the illegal use of passports. When questioned, he again denied he had ever been a member of the Communist Party but admitted he had in 1947 attended meetings where some communist writers had been present. When he refused to name these writers, he was cited for contempt of Congress, and when his case was brought on 15 February 1957, he was fined $500 and given a one-month suspended prison sentence. He appealed to the Supreme Court, and on 7 August 1958, he was acquitted on a legal technicality.

It is no coincidence that Miller should have been called to answer questions, as he had made Proctor stand before his accusers, and, like himself, 'refuse to repent'. His adaptation of Ibsen's play, *An Enemy of the People*, which had been produced in New York in 1950, then *The Crucible*, and, more directly, a satirical political essay, 'A Modest Proposal for the Pacification of the Public Temper', published in the *Nation* in 1954,had voiced his opinion on the mass hysteria and hypocrisy. Miller later wrote of the original, historical Proctor's 'evidently liberated cast of mind', and that 'he was one of the few who...persisted in calling the entire business a ruse and a fake'. The same could be said of Miller and his response to 'McCarthyism'. On the day of his acquittal, he made a formal statement to the Press which appeared in the *New York Times*. In it he said: 'The decision has made the long struggle of the past few years fully worthwhile...I can only hope that the decision will make some small contribution toward eliminating the excesses of Congressional committees, and particularly toward stopping the inhuman practice of making witnesses inform on long past friends and acquaintances.' In a previous statement to the *New York Herald Tribune* in January 1954, he had said: 'Nobody wants to be a hero. . .but in every man there is something he cannot give up and still remain himself – a core, an identity, a thing that is summed up for him by the sound of his own name on his own ears. If he gives that up, he becomes a different man, not himself.' This comment applies to both Miller and Proctor.

2.9 SUBSEQUENT WORK

While the McCarthy drama was being enacted, Miller was also involved in a personal drama which was avidly followed by the media. In June 1956 he divorced his first wife and immediately married Marilyn Monroe, a most popular, blonde film star. For her he wrote a film-script, *The Misfits*, which was released in 1961, the same year that this second marriage ended in divorce. In 1962 he married the photographer Ingeborg Morath, and with her he has published records of their travels: *In Russia* (1969), *In the Country* (1977) and *Chinese Encounters* (1979). A collection of short stories, *I Don't Need You Any More*, was published in 1967. His later plays include *After the Fall* (1964), *Incident at Vichy* (1964), *The Price* (1968), *Fame* (1970), *The Creation of the World, and Other Business* (1972), *Up from Paradise* (1974), *The Archibishop's Ceiling* (1977) and *The American Clock* (1980). A television script, *Playing for Time*, was presented in 1980.

The Crucible has remained Miller's most popular play, being performed all over the world. When 'McCarthyism' has been forgotten, and in times and places where the term is not even known, this play has something valuable to say to men and women who believe that the individual conscience overrules any political, religious or social dogma.

3 SUMMARIES AND CRITICAL COMMENTARY

3.1 PLOT SYNOPSIS

In Salem, Massachusetts, in 1692, a witch-hunt is started after a group of adolescent girls had been discovered by Parris, the parish minister, dancing and performing pagan rites with a negro slave, Tituba, in the forest. One of the girls, Abigail, had previously had an affair with a local farmer, John Proctor, and she had asked Tituba for a charm to kill John's wife, Elizabeth.

A court to find witches is set up in Salem, with the girls as chief witnesses. Once the witch-hunt has been set in motion, it is used as an excuse to pay back all the spite, envy, jealousy and guilt of the community, and in the resulting atmosphere of fear, bigotry and religious fervour, many innocent people are condemned to hang as witches.

Abigail had told Proctor that the girls' evidence was a fraud, and he tries to make another of the girls, Mary Warren, who is now his servant, confirm this in the court. But Abigail accuses Elizabeth of trying to kill her by making her 'familiar spirit' stick a needle in her belly, and Elizabeth is arrested as a witch. The only way John can expose Abigail is to admit his adultery and denounce her as a whore. But then, when she herself is accused of witchcraft by Abigail and the other girls, Mary Warren accuses Proctor of 'witching' her, and he is arrested.

Many people 'confess' to being in the service of the Devil rather than hang, but three of John's friends, Rebecca Nurse, and Giles and Martha Corey, refuse to confess to things they had not done. Elizabeth is given a year's reprieve because she is found to be pregnant. John at first 'confesses', but then tears up the confession he had signed and finds the strength to die rather than blacken his own name and that of his friends.

Abigail, meanwhile, has fled from the town for fear of a rebellion against the court.

NOTE This play is divided into four acts, but has no separate divisions into scenes within the acts. However, for convenience of study, the summaries

and commentaries consider the acts in manageable sections, breaking off at
natural divisions. In the first act, for example, the breaks are made at those
places where Arthur Miller interpolates his own commentaries. In this
section, only the play itself is considered, including the stage directions;
Miller's own comments on the background and characters are discussed,
as appropriate, in other sections of this book.

3.2 SUMMARIES AND COMMENTARY

Act 1 – to comments about Putnam

Summary

In a small upper bedroom of the house of the Reverend Samuel Parris in
Salem, Massachusetts in the spring of 1692, his daughter, Betty, aged ten,
is lying inert on the bed. Parris kneels by the bed in prayer. His negro slave,
Tituba, whom he had brought from Barbados, is anxious about Betty,
tries to enter, but is angrily ejected. His niece, Abigail Williams, a beautiful
girl of seventeen, enters to announce that Susanna Walcott has returned
from Doctor Griggs. Susanna enters and says the doctor can find no medi-
cine for Betty, but suspects unnatural things. Parris denies this, and says he
had sent for the Reverend Hale of Beverly. As she leaves, both Parris and
Abigail warn Susanna not to mention any 'unnatural causes'.

Abigail tells her uncle that there are rumours of witchcraft; he had
better go down and deny it to all the people assembled in the parlour
below. Parris reveals he had discovered Betty and Abigail dancing in the
forest, with Tituba waving her arms over a fire, and someone running
naked through the trees. Abigail admits the dancing and Tituba singing
songs from Barbados, but denies anyone was naked.

Parris, anxious to maintain his hard-won reputation in the parish,
questions Abigail about her reputation, and why she was discharged by
Goody Proctor. Abigail angrily denounces Elizabeth Proctor as a gossiping
liar.

Mrs Ann Putnam enters asking how high Betty flew, because Mr Collins
had seen her going over Ingersoll's barn. Parris is trying to deny this when
Mr Thomas Putnam enters, saying it is providence that the Devil's work is
now revealed. Their only child, Ruth, had been touched by the Devil and
lay senseless in bed with her eyes open. Mrs Putnam reminds Parris that
Hale had found a witch in Beverly, but Parris pleads that a charge of
witchcraft would have him driven out of Salem.

Commentary

Miller calls this first act 'An Overture'. It is setting a scene in which fear, guilt, hysteria, suspicion, accusations, hearsay, allegations and lies dominate the atmosphere.

The setting in the small upper bedroom means that the action is played out in a claustrophobic space, emphasising Parris's feeling of being trapped, with the 'parlour packed with people' downstairs representing a threat, much more menacing because it is unseen, except when representatives break into the bedroom. Notice that the window is 'narrow' and the furniture sparse. The 'raw and unmellowed' wood colours of the rafters are to remind the audience that this is a newly-established, 'raw' community – exposed rafters to a modern audience usually signal an old house and well-established community. The combination of morning sunlight and the candle still burning indicates that Parris's vigil had been going on all night.

The causes of Parris's anxiety are quickly revealed one by one: 'unnatural weeping, and his inert daughter on the bed, brings out his helplessness and worry, so when Tituba enters he lets out his anxiety in his fury against her. Tituba is genuinely concerned about Betty; Parris is more concerned for his own reputation; notice he says 'God help *me*!' not the child. He leans against the door to try to keep out the threat of the outside world. He pleads with Betty to wake, thinking more of his reputation than of the sick child.

This juxtaposition of contrasting emotions – anxiety, fear, love, fury – draws the audience into the emotional climate of the play.

Abigail, when she enters, is full of 'propriety' as well as 'worry' and 'apprehension'; this is part of her 'endless capacity for dissembling'; she can put on an act, or tell lies at will to gain what she wants, and she remains in control of any situation, as she is here with Parris.

The causes of Parris's anxiety are quickly revealed one by one: 'unnatural causes'; 'the rumour of witchcraft'; the threatening 'parlour packed with people'; his own daughter and niece 'discovered dancing like heathen in the forest'; his 'enemies', a faction sworn to drive him from his pulpit; Tituba waving her arms over the fire; the dress lying on the grass; and someone running naked through the trees. This last, to the Puritan Parris, was the greatest abomination, and although Abigail reacts to the 'dress on the grass' '*innocently*', she is '*in terror*' after the 'naked' accusation. But she quickly regains control by telling lies.

Notice the order in which Parris sees the threat: first his ministry; and then, perhaps, his daughter's life, and when he threatens Abigail with 'the weight of truth upon you' she answers, 'There is nothing more. I swear it, uncle', which, later in the act, we find is a lie. Abigail is astute enough to realise that Parris is concerned for the compromising of his 'very character' more than anything else, which is why she reacts 'with an edge of resentment' to any allegation about her character. Notice how she rises to '*temper*' after Goody Proctor is mentioned, and her words against Elizabeth could not be more bitter. We learn the reasons for this resentment later. Meanwhile, Abigail has succeeded in fending off Parris's inquisition, and even turning his accusations against himself.

Parris has to admit Mrs Ann Putnam because she is one of the chief 'stiff-necked people' whose good respect he had to keep, which is why 'a certain deference springs into him'. She arrives 'full of breath' and 'shiny-eyed' because she is full of gossip and rumour which she wants to turn against Parris with 'It is surely a stroke of hell upon you', and she accepts as fact the hearsay that Mr Collins had seen Betty flying over the barn.

The entry of Mr Putnam, to whom Parris has to be even more deferential, and the way he ignores Parris's greeting and goes straight to the bed, takes away any authority Parris had. Parris's over-emphatic denials – 'No – no' he repeats several times – only serve to show his doubt and anxiety; and that he is repeatedly interrupted by the Putnams, and is unable to finish his sentences, show how little respect they have for him. In contrast, both the Putnams come out with direct statements which appear to have the ring of authority, although all of them are based on hearsay, rumour and superstition.

Act 1 – to entry of Proctor

Summary

Mr Putnam tells Parris he must expose the witch who is laying a curse on the children. Mrs Putnam tells Parris she has lost seven babies and now Ruth was turning strange, so she had sent her to Tituba, who could speak to the dead, to find out who had murdered her babies. And now Ruth was struck dumb. Putnam tells Parris they have a murdering witch among them and he can hide it no longer; he can save himself by exposing the witchcraft in his house. Mercy Lewis, Putnam's servant, enters and says Ruth had improved a little after giving a powerful sneeze. Parris agrees to lead the people gathered in the parlour in a psalm, but he will not discuss witchcraft. Before he goes, with the Putnams, he warns Abigail not to let Betty get out of the window.

Left alone, Abigail and Mercy try to shake Betty into consciousness. In case she is questioned, Abigail tells Mercy what Parris already knows: that they danced; that Tituba conjured Ruth's sisters to come out of the grave; and that he saw Mary running naked. Mary Warren, the Proctor's servant, enters and says everyone is talking about witchcraft and they will be accused of being witches; she tells Abigail they must tell the truth and be whipped, not hanged as witches. When Betty whimpers on the bed, Abigail shakes her furiously, and tells her she had told her father everything. Betty, in a terrified delirium, calls for her dead mother, and tries to fly out of the window to her. Abigail restrains her, but when she repeats that she had told Betty's father everything, Betty says Abigail hadn't told him that she had drunk blood to kill Goody Proctor. Abigail viciously slaps Betty's face, and threatens them all that if they let out any hint that they had done more than dance and conjure Ruth's dead sisters, she would make them wish they had never been born. When Mary, in a hysterical fright, says Betty is going to die, and it's a sin to conjure, Abigail tells her to shut up, as John Proctor enters.

Commentary

Putnam, who has only contempt for him, pretends he has always tried to take Parris's part, but he is really trying to destroy him. Mrs Putnam's revelation that she had sent Ruth to Tituba to speak to the dead to find out who had 'murdered' her babies, shows her superstitious, vengeful spirit. As Parris warns her, it is a 'formidable sin to conjure up the dead', but Mrs Putnam, for revenge, is willing to take this sin on her soul if she can find out who murdered her babies, and she believes that Ruth was close to finding out before she also was silenced by the witch. (Ruth's 'turning strange' and becoming a 'secret child' is no more than usual adolescent behaviour with parents.) Putnam is convinced they have a witch among them, and, although he doesn't say it, he implies she is in Parris's house. Parris turns to Betty in terror because it is she, or Abigail, or Tituba, who by implication is being accused. There is the other possibility, that Betty herself had been struck by the witch. When Parris accuses Abigail of conjuring spirits, she coolly lies again, saying it had been only Tituba and Ruth. Putnam himself knows that he is lying when he tells Parris that he will not be 'undone' if he declares that he had discovered witchcraft in his own house; he knows perfectly well that Parris could never survive as the minister after this.

When Mercy enters, her 'Your pardons' is more insolent than polite. She is *sly* and *merciless* – which makes her name ironic. She has come to see how Betty is, but more to consult with Abigail; the situation is becoming more serious than they had expected. Her mention of the 'powerful sneeze' does bring a touch of reality into the proceedings. She knows the hysteria is self-induced, and thinks that Ruth and Betty can be shaken or beaten out of it.

Parris tries to get the Putnams to leave because he has had as much as he can stand. Abigail wants *him* to leave because she wants to discuss the situation with Mercy. With the accusation of witchcraft in the house, she is now frightened herself. Putnam's advice to Parris to 'strike out against the Devil, and the village will bless you for it' is completely hypocritical; he knows that many of the villagers are thirsting for Parris's blood. Parris's words to Putnam that there is 'terrible power' in Betty's arms, implies that he does believe that Betty is bewitched and could fly if she got out of the window. Such is the underlying superstitious belief of this minister.

When the girls are left alone, the atmosphere on the stage changes completely. The stage direction, *'with hushed trepidation'*, shows that Abigail is frightened by the turn in events, but she is still practical. That she thinks that Betty is putting on an act is shown by her words and actions when she turns to Betty. (Betty is probably suffering from shame and shock after her father 'leaped out of the bush so suddenly', which is more serious than Abigail had explained earlier. Her state is self-induced because she does not want to face her father.) Mercy's words, 'Have you tried beatin' her?' show how practical and merciless she is; but Abigail holds her back because she doesn't want any more abuse from her uncle.

Then Abigail's 'Listen now' shows she is in control again: if they are questioned they must agree on their answers, so she tells Mary the three things that Parris knows already; they will admit those and no more. Abigail and Mercy are strong and ruthless characters, but Mary Warren is *'a subservient, naïve, lonely girl'*, and therefore a weak link in the defence of themselves. When she says straight out, 'They'll be callin' us witches, Abby!', Mercy threatens her, as she does again when Mary tries to extricate herself from any responsibility by saying she 'only looked'.

When Betty whimpers, Abigail shows her ruthlessness by first pleading with 'Betty, dear'; then shaking her *'furiously'*; then threatening to beat her. But when Betty darts from the bed, the situation threatens to get out of control. Betty's efforts to fly to her Mama, in her hysterical state, were probably induced by what Mrs Putnam had said about her 'going over Ingersoll's barn'. But she soon shows she had heard and understood everything that had been going on in the room. When Abigail again tries to reassure her that her father knew everything that they had done, Betty comes out with the one thing that Abigail had concealed: Abigail had drunk blood as a charm to kill John Proctor's wife. This really frightens Abigail who 'smashes her across the face' and tells her to 'shut it!' This is a key revelation in the plot of the play: it has already been revealed that Abigail had been 'discharged from Goody Proctor's service', and Abigail had called her 'a bitter woman, a lying, cold, snivelling woman' and 'a gossiping liar'. But these are hardly enough reasons to want to kill her. In the next scene we find out why. But now she has to silence the other girls, apart from their agreed confessions, and there is no doubt that she could carry out her threats. Her speech is both practical and sinister. It begins with short, stabbing sentences to make them listen; it then has two long sentences, with blood-curdling threats, which include a piece of her own history which could, perhaps, explain her own ruthlessness. Then she deals roughly with Betty, now, partly, because she is frightened herself; and when Mary still shows hysterical fright, Abigail goes for her too.

At this dramatic moment, Proctor enters.

Act 1 – to Rebecca's calming of Betty

Summary
When Proctor enters, Mary and Mercy both leave. Left alone with Proctor, Abigail tries to attract him, mentioning the relationship between them when she worked at his farm, and saying he still lusted after her. When, in anger, she condemns his wife, he threatens her with whipping, but she asks him to pity her. The sound of the psalm is heard from below, and Betty (still on the bed) claps her hands to her ears and whines loudly. The Putnams, Mercy and Parris enter, and the Putnams say it is a clear case of witchcraft because Betty cannot bear to hear the name of Jesus in the psalm. Rebecca Nurse enters, soon followed by Giles Corey, whom she tells to keep quiet. And then Rebecca, by quietly standing by Betty, gradually calms her.

Commentary
From the tense, hysterical atmosphere that has been built up between the four girls, there is a complete change when Proctor enters. For a while, with his references to 'pay', 'cows' and 'work', and his sarcastic attitude to the 'great doings', he brings a breath of reality into the room – for the first time. But when he is left alone with Abigail, a new kind of intensity is built up again. We find out later that both Mercy and Mary know of Abigail's relationship with Proctor – which explains why they left so promptly.

This is a crucial scene, because it is Abigail's passion for Proctor, and, in spite of all his intentions and resolutions, his desire for her, that are key factors in the plot: she had been prepared to drink blood to destroy Proctor's wife; his desire makes him vulnerable because of his sense of guilt. In this scene, the actor playing Proctor has a very delicate task to project both his rejection of Abigail, but yet his attraction to her. His *'faintest suggestion of a knowing smile'* and then *'his smile widening'* when he says, 'Ah, you're wicked yet, aren't y'', are enough to suggest to Abigail – and to the audience – that she still attacts him; so his denial, 'No, no, Abby. That's done with', like Parris's repeated 'No, no' in the first scene, expresses doubt as much as strong denial. He cannot deny her so lightly, and he knows it.

Abigail's 'Gah! I'd almost forgot how strong you are, John Proctor' establishes her physical attraction to him, and her use of his Christian name establishes a familiarity between them. (Mary Warren would never call him 'John Proctor'.) The word 'Gah' is probably a corrupt form of 'God!', and it is possible for an actress to put an edge of feeling into this short exclamation, as can an actor, later, in John's 'Ah'. The stage directions show that Abigail is using all her wiles to try to win him back, and her words 'sweated like a stallion' show how physical the desire was on both sides. There is no evidence, as yet, that the physical relationship went further than his clutching her back behind the house; this is purposely left ambiguous by Miller, at this point in the play. The word 'more' in 'I'll not be comin' more' implies he had come to the town to be near her; and he admits 'I may have looked up' and 'I may think of you softly from time to time'. When he answers Abigail's taunt about his 'sickly wife', notice he is also angered *at himself as well* because he knows that it was because his wife left him sexually unsatisfied that he lusted after Abigail.

In her last plea to Proctor we still do not know whether he had, literally, taken her from her sleep, or if this was just her 'dream'; but the 'knowledge' her physical passion had given her made her scornful about the 'pretence' of Salem and 'these Christian women and their covenanted men'. (To be full members of the Church, Puritans must enter into a solemn covenant to accept its discipline, and marriage was seen as a similar covenant between a man and a woman.) That Abigail can treat with such scorn the whole basis of belief of this Puritan community shows where some of her strength lies. She is outside it all – and John, having broken his covenant with his wife, shows Abigail that he is outside it too. Her amoral position gives her power over everyone. So it is ironical that she uses a biblical phrase, 'tear the light out of my eyes', about this 'knowledge' she had gained through the physical love with John. Her last words: 'You loved me, John Proctor, and whatever sin it is, you love me yet!' are some of the truest words Abigail speaks in the whole play. Meanwhile, another ironic touch, during all this passionate speech, *a psalm is heard being sung below*, one of Miller's masterly off-stage devices.

During this whole passionate scene, Betty is forgotten; but she is still on the bed, presumably hearing everything, as she had in the previous scene. That Betty claps her ears and whines loudly at the words 'going up to Jesus' is purposely left ambiguous. Was it these words, or Abigail's words, that Betty could not stand any longer? Notice that even Proctor is *growing unnerved* by Betty's hysterics. Abigail, of course, not wanting to disclose what had been said between herself and Proctor, says it was the singing that had caused Betty to scream, and the Putnams immediately jump to the conclusion that suits them as it was another sign of witch-craft.

Rebecca Nurse brings a calm feeling of sanity into the room, and her warning to Giles Corey to keep quiet when he enters shows that she knows that even he is affected by the mass hysteria, as his words about flying show. But Rebecca, by doing no more than quietly standing over the child, quietens her. The audience should feel, at this point, that with such people as Rebecca around, there is still a possibility of hope for this community.

Act 1 – to entry of the Reverend John Hale

Summary
Having calmed Betty, to the Putnams' and Parris's astonishment, Rebecca asks them to calm themselves. She had eleven children and twenty-six grandchildren, and knows that children go through a 'silly season', but come out of it when they are ready. She hopes Mr Parris will not 'decide to go in search of loose spirits'. Proctor accuses Parris and Putnam of sending for Hale without calling a meeting. Rebecca tells Proctor to be calm, and thinks they should rely on the doctor and prayer, and blame themselves. But the contention continues between Parris, Proctor and Putnam, with Giles joining in: about Putnam trying to order Parris; Proctor not coming to church; Parris preaching about Hell and not God; Parris not getting his firewood; about obedience to the Church. When Putnam says there is a faction against Parris and all authority, Proctor says he wants to find it, and asks Giles to join him. Rebecca tries to keep the peace. When Proctor says he must go to drag lumber home, another argument arises about Putnam's grandfather willing away other people's land. Just as Proctor and Giles are about to leave, the Reverend John Hale enters.

Commentary
The Putnams, although '*astonished*', think Rebecca's calming of Betty is some kind of magical trick, which Mr Putnam wants her to try on Ruth. Rebecca treats the whole business in a matter-of-fact, common-sense way, but the mention of all her children and grandchildren only arouses jealousy and envy in the Putnams who want to find the witch who 'murdered' their babies, whose deaths Rebecca is unable to explain.

The decision of Parris and Mr Putnam to send for Hale to look for devils, brings out all the contention, the malicious spite, jealousy, suspicions and accusations in the community. (The Puritan community was supposed to be a peace-loving, democratic society where decisions were reached by agreement at meetings of senior members or warders). Now Proctor accuses Parris of sending for Hale without calling a meeting, and then accuses Putnam of trying to order people about because he is a big landowner. Rebecca vainly tries to keep the peace, but once the arguments have started, all the petty spites come out.

This scene is important because it makes the 'contention' real, and it is against this background that the chances for revenge arise amongst the members of the community. But Proctor already shows himself to be a dangerous man by questioning 'authority' and by 'speaking his heart'.

Act 1 - to comment by Giles

Summary

Hale enters, loaded down with heavy books. He immediately identifies Rebecca, although he had never seen her before, because she looks such a good soul. Parris introduces him to Mr and Mrs Putnam who ask him to help with Ruth. When Hale asks Proctor and Giles Corey if they have sick children, Corey says Proctor doesn't believe in witches, but Proctor says he has never spoken one way or the other. Proctor leaves, saying he hopes Hale will bring some sense into Salem, but Corey says he wants to stay.

Parris takes Hale to look at Betty, saying she had tried to fly. When Putnam says that is a sure sign of witchcraft, Hale denies this. They agree to abide by his judgement. Parris tells of the girls dancing in the forest, and Mrs Putnam adds that she had sent Ruth to Tituba to conjure up the dead. Rebecca is horrified by this, but Mrs Putnam says that to lose seven children at birth is not natural. Hale is impressed by this, and goes to his books which he says will disclose the Devil in any shape, and says he will crush him if he is amongst them. Rebecca is anxious for Betty, and leaves, saying she is going to pray to God. Putnam is anxious to proceed, but now Giles breaks in to tell Hale that he cannot pray when his wife is reading her books.

Commentary

Hale's entrance is the first real introduction of any humour into the play. His heavy books, 'weighted with authority', cannot but help raise a smile. Like an earnest intellectual, he thinks he can find the answers to any problem in his books; but it is significant that he immediately recognises Rebecca, who, because of her essential goodness and common sense, is the only 'authority' who could have solved their problems, had they listened to her.

Parris, still being obsequious, is anxious to introduce the Putnams; they, selfishly, want Hale to concentrate his attentions on their daughter. When Proctor is introduced, Giles Corey, a naïve but honest person, cannot help letting out what he must have heard Proctor say at one time - but Proctor, neither quite so naïve nor honest, protests an open mind on the question of witches. When he leaves, saying he hopes Hale will leave some of his sense in Salem, his implication is clear: in his opinion, there isn't much sense around in some of the present company. This is immediately proved by seemingly rational people discussing Betty's attempt to fly as if it were factually possible. Even Hale, whom Proctor had called 'sensible', has no doubt about the Devil's existence. There is no 'superstition' involved; and on this basis of belief in the Devil being precise, they agree to his judgement.

When Hale begins his investigation, the dancing of the girls comes out, and Mrs Putnam, who *knows* that Tituba has knowledge of conjuring, cannot resist revealing she had sent her child to find out from Tituba who had murdered the babies. This involvement of a child in black magic horrifies Rebecca, who is the only person primarily concerned for the children, as she shows later with her question about Betty being hurt. Rebecca has already given her opinion on what was wrong with the children, and she doesn't want to see the 'ripping and tearing' to get Betty free. When she leaves, saying she is 'going to God', Parris takes this to mean that she implies they are going to Satan. Notice that they all *'feel resentful of her note of moral superiority'*.

Hale, meanwhile, had been impressed by the story of seven children dead in childbirth, and goes to his books for information. Miller intends the audience to laugh at him here, with his *'tasty love of intellectual pursuit'*, but his words 'Have no fear now' are cruelly ironic. They are just what cause Rebecca to fear, and to leave; she doesn't want to be associated with this superstitious 'authority'.

Putnam, *'abruptly'*, wants Hale to get on with it, but before he can, Giles Corey comes out with his particular brand of superstition – his suspicion of books. For him it is a fear of the unknown, because he, like most of these people, is illiterate. Hale, in spite of attempting to remain detached, has already been drawn into the superstitious fears of these people.

Notice that Abigail, although she has not spoken, has been present, listening, during the last two scenes.

Act 1 – to end of act

Summary
For the time being, Hale puts aside Giles' concern that he cannot pray while his wife is reading, and turns again to attempt to rouse Betty. When she remains inert, he turns to question Abigail. She admits they were dancing, and that a very little frog had jumped into the soup in the kettle. She names Tituba, and when she is brought in, Abigail immediately accuses her of making her drink blood, laugh during prayers, and dream corruptions. Threatened with whipping to death by Parris, and hanging by Putnam, Tituba is terrified. When Hale asks her who came with the Devil to visit her, Putnam suggests Sarah Good, and Goody Osburn. Further questioned by Hale, Tituba admits the Devil had told her to kill Parris, but she had resisted. But the Devil revealed that some white people belonged to him, and she names Sarah Good and Goody Osburn. When Hale tells Tituba that God will bless her for her help, Abigail 'confesses' her pact with the Devil, and 'names' Sarah Good and Bridget Bishop. Betty then rises from the bed and 'names' George Jacobs and Goody Howe. As the

hysteria rises, with more people being accused, Hale calls for the marshal to bring irons.

Commentary

Giles persists with his suspicions about his wife's reading, but Hale will not be detracted from his concern with Betty; he immediately shows his own superstitious gullibility by warning against the 'frightful wonders', and asking Mr Putnam to 'stand close in case she flies'. When he sits Betty up, and *'the others watch breathlessly'*, the audience are drawn in to watch breathlessly too. But his 'Hmmm' begins to bring an element of farce into the proceedings: for all his *'heavy books'*, he cannot understand the simple truth about what is wrong with the child, as Rebecca with her common sense had done.

The dramatic intensity, tinged with the edge of farce, increases with Hale's introduction of the 'bird', 'pig' or 'mouse'. The audience is in the ambiguous position of wanting to know how Betty is going to react, but at the same time amused that seemingly rational people could believe such superstitious nonsense. The intoning of the Latin brings the session with Betty fittingly to a close with a piece of solemn nonsense which, however, impresses the characters on stage.

After the purposely slow pace of this scene, where the characters (and the audience) wait for Betty to react when Hale turns to Abigail, the action rapidly gains momentum until the climax of hysteria at the end of the act. Notice the stage direction *'his eyes narrowing'*. Hale had enough understanding of human nature to recognise Rebecca Nurse for her essential goodness; he now realises that the source of the trouble is Abigail. Parris again brings in an element of farce with the kettle, which leads to the inquisition about what was in it. Live spiders, mice, frogs, and so on were supposed to be common ingredients of the brew that witches concocted in their cauldrons (see, for example, in Shakespeare's play *Macbeth*). Abigail tries, weakly, to evade the inquisition by admitting that 'a very little frog' did jump into the pot, but even she must have realised this was a most unlikely story, so, when Hale accuses her of calling the Devil, she realises the best way to save herself is to blame someone else, and names Tituba. But her fear that things are getting out of control is shown by her attempt to make Betty wake up.

When Tituba appears, Abigail instantly points at her to take the pressure away from herself; but notice that Tituba is genuinely *'shocked and angry'* to be accused by Abigail because, as Tituba later makes clear (and there is no reason to doubt her word) it was Abigail who had begged her to conjure and make a charm.

Tituba's part in this scene needs careful consideration. As Miller said earlier *'her slave sense has warned her that, as always, trouble. . . eventually lands on her back'*. She is *'shocked and angry'* when Abigail accuses her, because it was Abigail who had begged her to 'conjure'. But now that Abigail is herself accused, she escapes by blaming Tituba for all her evil deeds, thoughts and dreams. Tituba is justified in being shocked and angry, because she knows that Abigail doesn't really believe what she is saying about Tituba; she is telling lies to shift the blame from herself, and pur- posely playing up to the superstitious beliefs of Hale, Parris and Putnam.

Parris, in his fear for his own position, and Putnam in his desire for revenge against somebody, both threaten Tituba with death, and Tituba, *'terrified'*, now blames 'somebody else'.

Hale's scene with Betty had been an anticlimax; but now his scene with Tituba has great dramatic intensity. More and more pressure is put on Tituba: first by being threatened with death; then by having to look into Hale's eyes; then by Hale taking her hand (which surprises her); then by Parris *'pressing in on her'*. She is basically a good but simple woman, her paganism overlaid with a simplistic form of Christianity where God = good, and the Devil = evil. The evil thoughts she had had, such as the desire to kill Parris (natural enough for a slave with such a master) she attributes to the Devil; and now, in her extremity, she *'suddenly burst out'* and confesses these evil thoughts. But the other evil thought she had had was that some white people were in league with the Devil, and although, previously, she had evaded accusing anyone, she now 'names' the two that Putnam had put into her head, giving back what she thought he wanted to hear.

When Abigail realises that Tituba has escaped the pressure on herself by 'opening' herself and naming others, she is *'inspired'* to do the same. Tituba, under extreme pressure and terrified for her life, reacting to the suggestions of others, had started the witch-hunt; Abigail then, deliber- ately, gives it momentum, and Betty joins in, all to detract blame from themselves. (Had Betty been conscious all this time? Notice she calls out *'with great relief'*.)

So the act ends on a rising note of hysteria with the ominous note sounded by Hale's, 'Let the marshal bring irons!'

Act 2 – to entry of Mary Warren

Summary
It is eight days later, at Proctor's farm some miles outside the town. Before Elizabeth enters, Proctor tastes, and then adds some more salt to, the stew over the fire. There is constraint between the two. Elizabeth suspects he has been in Salem, and he knows she thinks he had been to see Abigail. She tells him that their servant girl, Mary Warren, now 'an official of the court', had been and told her of the court in Salem, with fourteen people

in jail, and the promise of hanging if they didn't confess. Abigail and the other girls were in court, and if they screamed and howled and fell on the floor when someone was brought before them, then that person was clapped in jail for bewitching them.

Elizabeth tells her husband he must go to town and tell the court that Abigail had told him it was not witchcraft. Proctor says he must think about it, and reveals he has no witness because he had been alone with Abigail when she had told him (whereas, previously, he had led Elizabeth to believe there had been other people present). Elizabeth says he wouldn't hesitate if it were anyone other than Abigail he had to expose as a fraud. Proctor tells his wife not to judge him, but she says his own heart judges him (for his affair with Abigail).

Commentary

Although the room in Proctor's house is *'low and dark'*, the *'fields outside'* and the gun which he carries when he enters bring some feeling of the great 'outside' into the room, as later do the mention of the 'forest edge', 'the farm is seeded', the 'load of flowers on the earth', and the 'lilacs'. Proctor is revealed as a man who appreciates sensuous beauty, whereas Elizabeth, who had not brought flowers into the room, and had forgotten the cider, is shown as sensuously cold. As Proctor says at the end of the scene, 'Your justice would freeze beer.' His tasting of the stew, being 'not quite pleased', and then adding an extra pinch of salt, and finally saying 'It's well seasoned', encapsulates the relationship between the two: he wishes she were a bit more 'salty'; she 'takes great care' to try to please him, but yet doesn't; he is well-intentioned, but nevertheless dishonest. By these small, symbolic actions, Miller has established the unsatisfactory sexual relationship between husband and wife, which is at the heart of Proctor's part in the play. Proctor's words, 'It's winter in here yet' are also symbolic of the cold relationship between them, which is brought out by the disjointed dialogue, with Elizabeth's brief replies and the frequent pauses. Then the reason for Elizabeth's apprehension emerges; she thinks he is late returning because she suspects he had been to Salem, and he knows she thinks this was to see Abigail.

The report from Mary Warren, whom the sudden power given to the girls had changed from a 'mouse' to being 'like the daughter of a prince', is used to bring news to Proctor (and the audience) of the setting up of the court and its consequences. That eight days had passed and the news had not reached the farm previously, serves to show how isolated the Proctors were. It then emerges that Proctor had told his wife what Abigail had said about the 'witchcraft', but had lied in saying they were 'with a crowd' when she told him. To Elizabeth it is clear that John should go immediately to town to expose the fraud; but when he prevaricates, it then emerges that he had been alone with Abigail. She then loses '*all faith in him*', and openly accuses him that he wouldn't hesitate if it were not Abigail that he had to expose. But when Proctor says '*with solemn warning*' that he has to think before he accuses Abigail of fraud, he is fearing that Abigail would 'name' Elizabeth as a witch.

Elizabeth's simple words, 'And I' are difficult to understand. Does she mean that she also has forgotten Abigail, which she obviously hasn't because the girl is dominant in her thoughts; or does she mean that her husband has forgotten her also?

But now the tension, and the feeling of guilt there had been in the household since Abigail had been dismissed, comes out into the open.

Act 2 – to exit of Mary Warren

Summary
When Mary enters, Proctor vents some of his anger on her, but her strangeness puts him off. She gives Elizabeth a small rag doll she says she had made in Court. She tells them thirty-nine were now arrested and Goody Osburn was condemned by the Deputy Governor to hang because she 'condemned herself' by not being able to repeat the Ten Commandments. Sarah Good had escaped hanging by confessing her pact with the Devil. When Proctor threatens Mary with a whip, the girl says she had saved Elizabeth's life that day.

Commentary
This scene demonstrates the power of the action that had been started in Salem; John and Elizabeth, two of the strongest characters in the play, are unable to gain the upper hand over Mary, who is one of the weakest characters, because of the power invested in her by the court.

The 'poppet' she gives Elizabeth is to play an important part later in the act, which brings ironic hypocrisy to Mary's words, 'We must all love each other now, Goody Proctor', because it is through the evidence of this poppet that Elizabeth is later accused.

Proctor's shock at the actions of the court is heightened by Mary not only confirming his fears, but showing they had been rapidly overtaken; there were not fourteen women accused, but thirty-nine; and not only would the Deputy Governor allow Goody Osburn to hang, it was he who had condemned her. This shows how out of touch Proctor is.

Mary then gives a graphic, first-hand demonstration of how an irrational minor fear and sense of guilt can lead, in this atmosphere, to enough 'evidence' to condemn a person to death: Mary's sense of guilt at sending Sarah away 'empty', led her to suspect that Sarah's 'mumblings' were some kind of curse, and this, by auto-suggestion, led her to fear that Goody Osburn was trying to kill her. There is no 'proof' at all that Sarah Osburn in any way caused Mary to 'fall sick'; and that she could not recite the Commandments is no proof of her guilt either. And Sarah Good, being declared pregnant at the age of sixty, is the final piece of nonsense, once again bordering on farce. It would be funny if it were not so menacingly serious.

And then, at the end of this scene, the source of Mary's strength over Proctor and his wife comes out: she had had Elizabeth's life in her hands. Although they think the whole thing is 'mad', they know they are in danger.

Act 2 – to entry of Hale

Summary

Elizabeth knows that it was Abigail who had 'mentioned' her because the girl wanted her dead and to take her place as Proctor's wife. Abigail would not dare to name such a respectable woman as Elizabeth unless she stood to gain much from it; and by his sexual relationship with Abigail, John had made her a 'promise'. Elizabeth wants him to go and denounce Abigail as 'a whore', and so break the 'promise', but when he shows unwillingness, she realises that, even against his will, Abigail still has some hold over him.

Commentary

This short scene is important for understanding the relationship between John, Elizabeth and Abigail. Although John had said earlier that he had 'forgot' Abigail, he had never shown her any contempt, and, from the evidence of the short scene between John and Abigail in the first act, it is clear that Elizabeth is better at 'understanding young girls' than is her husband: Abigail's words in that scene, 'I have something better than hope, I think', show that she still saw a 'promise' in the sexual relationship she had had with John, and this could not be broken until John deliberately broke it by denouncing Abigail and calling her a whore. And that Abigail, like one of Cupid's darts, still 'has an arrow' in John, is shown by his using exactly the same image about his relationship with Abigail as she has used in the earlier scene: she had said, 'You sweated like a stallion when I came near!'; and now he says, 'The promise that a stallion gives a mare I gave that girl.' But it was this physical, 'stallion', sexual part of him that he had to repress with his wife, but which Abigail, with her own 'wicked' wild nature, had satisfied. That Proctor is not entirely 'honest', and is capable of 'deceit', we have seen earlier in this act with the salting of the stew.

Act 2 – to entry of Giles

Summary

The revealing dialogue between husband and wife is broken off by the sudden, silent and unexpected arrival of Hale. He tells them that Elizabeth had been 'mentioned' in court, which they already know. He then mentions Rebecca Nurse, and when they protest her piety, Hale says that although he had no doubt that the 'powers of the dark' had attacked the village, Rebecca would not be accused.

He then turns to question them about the 'Christian character' of their house. Why had Proctor been to church only twenty-six times in seventeen months? Why had only two of their three sons been baptised? Proctor says his wife had been sick, and he didn't like Parris replacing the pewter candlesticks with gold ones. And he didn't like Parris to touch his baby because he 'saw no light of God in the man'. Hale says this is not for Proctor to decide, and there is a 'softness' in his record. He then asks them to repeat the Commandments – and John, by a Freudian slip, forgets 'adultery' – until prompted by Elizabeth. Hale says this is a 'crack in the fortress of religion'.

When, with obvious misgivings, he is about to leave, Elizabeth prompts John to tell Hale what Abigail had told him about the witchcraft being a fraud. When Hale asks why he had never revealed this before, Proctor says he had not until then known that the world had 'gone daft'. This affronts Hale because he says many had confessed to dealing with the Devil, and when Proctor says that a person condemned to hang will confess anything, he has to agree. When Hale asks Proctor if he will testify in court, John hesitates because he is made wary when such a 'steady-minded minister' as Hale could suspect such a woman as Elizabeth (or Rebecca Nurse?). Hale then asks them if they believe in witches as the Bible speaks of them. John prevaricates, but Elizabeth says she cannot believe, which shocks Hale. She tells him to question Abigail about the Gospel. Hale is about to leave, telling them to have their third child baptised and to go to church each Sunday, when Giles enters, followed by Francis Nurse.

Commentary

The sudden appearance of Hale, *'as though from the air'*, is meant to shock the audience as well as the Proctors. He catches them off their guard, and adds to the threat they feel. John, notice, still has the gun in his hand. Although *'there is a quality of deference'* in Hale's manner now, nevertheless, because of the shock he caused them at such a critical moment, he starts off with the initiative. Although Proctor quickly overcomes his shock and is polite, asking Hale to sit, and offering him cider, it is Hale who asks the other two to sit before he begins his business. His simple words, 'Hear me', and the wetting of his lips, serve to calm the tempo, but it is quickly disrupted again at the mention of Rebecca Nurse (whom, remember, Hale had himself recognised for her essential goodness). So when Hale says it is possible that she had 'trafficked with the Devil', both the Proctors lose faith in Hale, even though he says he knows she will not be accused. (He is wrong here, too.) So when Hale starts asking Proctor about the Christian character of his house, he is *cold and resentful*.

The exact numbers that Hale quotes for Proctor's attendances at church show that Parris had been complaining to Hale about Proctor, and this is later confirmed when Hale asks why only two of his sons had been baptised. Proctor's resentment and dislike of Parris then comes out in his accusing Parris of wanting golden candlesticks, and the straight judgement: 'I see no light of God in the man.' Although, from a common-sense point of view, Hale probably agrees with Proctor, nevertheless Proctor's 'theology' should tell him that he should go to church to pray, and that if Parris is ordained, *therefore*, the light of God must be in him. It is Proctor's questioning of these accepted tenets of the ruling theology, later brought out in their refusal to accept the existence of witches, that bring both the Proctors into conflict with the authorities. And that Proctor 'nailed the roof upon the church and hung the door', is a 'good sign', but not necessarily proof of his faith.

Hale then turns to ask them the same question that they know Goody Osburn had been asked in court – and condemned to hang because she couldn't answer. When asked to recite the Commandments, although John says, 'I – am sure I do, sir', notice he is a *'a trifle unsteady'* and he is *'beginning to sweat'*. This is a tense moment for the audience as well, because although they know this is no true test of a devout Christian, they want John to complete the Commandments. But the one he forgets is, significantly, adultery, the very one he had committed. When Elizabeth prompts him, notice the stage direction *'as though a secret arrow had pained his heart'*. Although Proctor tries to *'grin it away'*, his words, 'I think it be a small fault' are ironic because although his forgetting one Commandment is a small fault, his adultery is not. Later in the act he comes to see his adultery as the 'crack in the fortress' that has started the madness in their community. 'Think on your village,' Hale says at the end of the act, 'and what may have drawn from heaven such thundering wrath upon you all.'

Hale is about to leave, still believing in the 'godly wisdom of the court', when Elizabeth is unable to restrain herself from attempting to take the suspicion away from herself by making John tell Hale about what Abigail had said. But although Hale is *'struck'*, with *'his eyes wide'*, by Abigail's saying it had nothing to do with witchcraft, he is *'suspicious'* as to why Proctor had not revealed this before. And he is offended when Proctor dismisses the whole business as 'nonsense', his proof being that several of the condemned women had confessed to 'dealing with the Devil'. When Proctor asks him if he had ever thought that some people would swear to anything before they hang, there is an important stage direction to help understand Hale's position: '*It is his own suspicion, but he resists it.*'

When Hale asks him if he will testify in court, Proctor still hesitates, but now, if such a 'steady minded minister as Hale' (is he being sarcastic?) can have suspicions about such a pious woman as Elizabeth (or Rebecca), then he has cause to falter. Hale then comes out with the 'rumour' he had heard about Proctor – that he doesn't believe in witches. (It was Giles Corey who had voiced this 'rumour' in the first act.) Proctor, '*striving against his disgust with Hale and with himself for even answering*', tries to prevaricate; but Elizabeth, with her direct honesty, shocks Hale by saying outright that she cannot believe if he thinks she could possibly be a witch. Hale again holds up the Gospel as his authority, and Elizabeth again turns her scorn on to Abigail.

Hale, now with his suspicions confirmed, and his own doubts increased, is about to leave them with the admonition to have their third child baptised and to go to church each Sunday, when Giles Corey, quickly followed by Francis Nurse, appears to prove that Hale had been wrong about Rebecca not being accused.

Act 2 – to end of act

Summary

Giles says his wife had been taken, and when Francis Nurse enters, he says that Rebecca was in jail too for 'the supernatural murder of Goody Putnam's babies'. Francis appeals to Hale, who tells him to rely on the court, and when Proctor intervenes angrily on Rebecca's account, Hale says that before he fell, Satan was one of the brightest angels in Heaven. Giles says his wife was taken because a man called Walcott, who had bought a pig from her, which died, had charged her with bewitching his pigs with her books.

Ezekiel Cheever then enters, followed by Marshal Herrick. Giles tells Ezekiel he will burn in Hell for what he is doing, but Cheever says he must do as he is told, and produces a warrant for the arrest of Elizabeth. She had been charged by Abigail, and the court had bid him search for any poppets in the house. Elizabeth, forgetting the one given her by Mary, denies she has any, but Cheever sees the poppet on the mantel, and tries to take Elizabeth. Proctor resists and tells Elizabeth to fetch Mary. Meanwhile Cheever lifts the poppet's skirt and, astonished, finds a needle stuck in its belly. When Hale asks what this means, he says that Abigail, sitting at dinner with Parris, had fallen to the floor screaming, and revealed a needle stuck in her belly, put there, she had said, by Elizabeth's 'familiar spirit'. When Proctor appeals to Hale that Abigail could have done it herself, Hale remains silent, *'struck by the proof'*, as is Cheever.

When Mary enters, frightened, she evasively explains how the poppet came to be in the house, that she believed she stuck the needle in, and how Abigail was sitting next to her when she made it. Hale asks her if someone (Elizabeth?) is not conjuring her to say this, but she denies this. Then Hale says this means that Mary is charging Abigail with murder (in charging Elizabeth as a witch for something she had not done), but then tells Elizabeth that she is charged with sticking a needle in Abigail's belly. Elizabeth exclaims that Abigail is 'murder' and 'must be ripped out of the world'. Cheever takes this as further proof of Elizabeth's guilt. Proctor rips up the warrant and orders them out of his house.

Hale still pleads the authority of the court. Proctor asks Hale why he doesn't wonder if the accusers are without guilt. Elizabeth realises she must go, and when Hale still says the court is 'just', Proctor calls him Pontius Pilate. Elizabeth gives instructions to John about the house and children, and he says he will bring her home. When she goes, and the sound of chains is heard outside, Proctor rushes out, but Herrick pushes him back saying he is under orders to chain them.

Giles accuses Hale for his silence, saying he knows it is fraud. Hale tries to plead charity with Proctor, who accuses him of being a coward. Hale then says, before he goes, there must be some secret abomination done in the village for such wrath to fall on them. Hale's words cause Proctor to think of his adultery with Abigail, and he asks Giles and Francis to leave. (Francis must leave here although there is no stage direction in the text for him.)

Left with Mary, Proctor tells her she must come to court with him and tell who had stuck the needle in the poppet. Mary says Abigail will kill her if she charges her with murder, and then reveals that Abigail had told her of Proctor's lechery and will charge him with it. Proctor says, bitterly, that she is no longer a saint then, and they will fall together. The truth was now out, and his wife would not die for him.

Commentary

For the second time, Hale is about to leave when he is further detained by the entrance of Giles and Francis. Not only Hale, but also the audience, are caught by the revelations they bring. The action now moves towards the dramatic climax to this act.

Hale is particularly implicated by the arrest of Rebecca, because not only had he recognised her 'as such a good soul' on his first arrival, but he had just told the Proctors she would not be accused. But now, although *'deeply troubled'*, he still falls back on the justice of the court, believing that there is proof that 'the Devil is alive in Salem'. By his example of the Devil (Satan), who right up to the moment of his fall was one of the brightest angels in Heaven, he is saying, by implication, that Rebecca could be the same. But Rebecca being charged for the 'supernatural murder' of Mrs Putnam's babies is such obvious envious spite; and Walcott's charge of Martha Corey for bewitching his pigs with her books such ignorant nonsense; it is a five-year-old grudge seeking revenge. The hysterical atmosphere that has been whipped up in the community is now being used to pay old scores.

However, none of this can be discussed because of the dramatic entry of Cheever, quickly followed by Herrick. These two represent the petty officials in any society who are willing to commit any atrocity against their neighbours because they feel they must do as they are told by the authorities. Cheever says 'I must do as I'm told', and Herrick, later, 'I cannot help myself. I must chain them' - because he had been told to do so. Cheever is quite proud of the power that is given him by the 'tonnage of the law' carried on his back; but Herrick is more *shamefaced*' and, although he must do his duty as marshal, he remains more impersonal.

That Elizabeth first denies she has any poppet - when it is there on the mantel; then the finding of the needle; then her saying that Abigail must be ripped out of the world, has a kind of logic to it that convinces Cheever of her guilt. But the probable true explanation of events emerges from what Mary says: Abigail sat next to Mary in court while she was making the poppet; told her to give it to Elizabeth; stuck a needle in its belly; stuck a needle in herself while having dinner with Parris; then blamed Elizabeth's 'familiar spirit'. It is a common belief in witchcraft that if you make an image of your enemy and stick pins in it, the injury can be transferred to the enemy. Abigail has already shown herself passionate and determined enough to inflict this wound on herself. And Mary's hesitant reply when asked if she stuck the needle in herself - 'I - believe I did, sir, I -' - shows that she knows that Abigail did it, knows its significance because Abigail had told her about John Proctor, but is afraid to confess because of her fear of Abigail.

Hale is also, at first, struck by the proof of the needle, but when Mary gives her account and says she is 'entirely herself', he realises the significance - that if what Mary is saying is true, then Abigail was attempting to murder Elizabeth by having her falsely charged as a witch. But Elizabeth's intervention, and Proctor's angry tearing up of the warrant, stop any further questions, and Hale goes back to the justice of the court. Then Proctor, in his anger, comes out with one of the key questions: why are only the accusers innocent, especially when it is evident that the law is being used for vengeance?

Elizabeth, with her usual common sense, even in this situation, realises she must go, and calmly tries to give Mary and her husband instructions about the house and children, but *'cannot go on'*. Although the audience had heard of women being taken before (including Rebecca and Martha), this is the first time that the separation of a woman from her home, children and husband is enacted on the stage, and the result, particularly because Elizabeth has been established as a good, honest woman, is shattering. But then the pain is heightened by one of Miller's most telling off-stage noises – *'the clank of chains'*, and the audience, as well as Proctor, knows what is happening.

Hale, notice, is *'in a fever of guilt and uncertainty'*, but he proves himself to be like Pontius Pilate by turning away to avoid the sight. But in his extremity – and Proctor is correct to call him a coward – he comes out with two pertinent points: that Proctor lays the blame for the 'world going mad' on the vengeance of 'a little girl' (that is, Abigail, who is certainly more than a 'little girl'); and that all the thundering wrath brought upon their village must be the result of some secret abomination that stinks to Heaven. Proctor *'has been reached by Hale's words'* and his sense of guilt for his adultery with Abigail is now brought home to him. He started the train of events which led to Elizabeth's arrest. Then, as a final blow, when Mary, to defend herself, lets him know that Abigail had told her about his lechery, his attempts at self-deceit fall apart.

Act 3 – to entry of Proctor with Mary Warren

Summary
The curtain rises on the vestry ante-room of the Salem Meeting House. From the general court in the adjacent hall, Judge Hathorne is heard accusing Martha Corey of telling fortunes. Giles' voice, shouting out that he has evidence they are hearing lies, causes an uproar. Giles is half-carried into the vestry by Herrick; followed by Hale, who tells Giles to be calm; then by Hathorne, who blames Giles for the uproar; then by Deputy Governor Danforth, Cheever and Parris. Giles, weeping and ashamed, tries to tell Danforth that he had not meant to condemn his wife by saying she read books. He is gently pushed out by Herrick. Francis Nurse, whose wife Rebecca, Hale says, was condemned that morning, tells Danforth that he is deceived because they have evidence that the girls are frauds.

Commentary
Once again, as in the first act, the scene is set in a room adjacent to a bigger room (off-stage) where, it is supposed, many more people are gathered than just those who appear on the stage. This gives the audience two impressions: that the people they see are only a small representative group

of a much wider community (and the numbers given for those arrested confirm this); the second is to focus more concentratedly on those people we do see, both as symbolising the historical victims, judges, intermediaries, and also to personalise, and so make more dramatic and tragic, all the abstract qualities that are enacted in the play – vengeance, spite, envy, intolerance, deceit, hypocrisy, pig-headedness, guilt, as well as honesty, common sense, bravery, fear, etc. The *'solemn'* and *'forbidding'* appearance of the room, with its heavy beams jutting out and its walls with *'boards of random widths'* establishes the harsh, primitive and unsophisticated conditions in which these people lived. But notice the *'sunlight pouring through two high windows'*: the sun shining outside, and all that it symbolises, makes the madness being enacted in these rooms, by contrast, even darker.

An empty stage always raises the expectations of the audience: who is going to come on to it? The few questions of Hathorne to Martha establish that the courtroom is next door, and the roar after Corey's interruption, that many people are in court. An atmosphere of tense excitement and some confusion is established even before so many characters, in quick succession, come pouring on to the stage.

Giles' blunt honesty and his lack of respect for people in authority (although there is a certain deference towards Danforth) is shown by his words to Herrick, Hale, Hathorne and Parris; but a new, pathetic side to him is shown by his concern for his wife, particularly because it is his own words about her books that contributed to her being charged. His blunt, direct statements, his unexpected *'helpless sobs'* and his sense of shame have a tragic and honest ring: 'They'll be hanging my wife!'; 'I have broke charity with the woman, I have broke charity with her'. For all his coarse rudeness and contentiousness, he is, underneath, a man with a feeling and honest heart.

Then Francis Nurse (who probably entered with Giles, though again there is no stage direction for him) also shows his direct honesty, very respectfully but bravely, by refusing to be silenced and telling Danforth that he was deceived, that they have evidence the girls were frauds.

The difference between the two judges, Hathorne and Danforth, is quickly established by their reactions to Francis: Danforth is at least willing to listen; Hathorne wants to treat comment on, or question of, authority as contempt.

Act 3 – to entry of Putnam

Summary
Giles re-enters with Proctor, supporting Mary Warren, who tells Danforth that the seeing of spirits was all a pretence. Parris tells Danforth that

Proctor wants to overthrow the court, but Danforth asks Proctor if his purpose is to save his wife. Parris tells Danforth that Proctor seldom comes to church, and Cheever tells how he tore up the warrant and that he ploughs on Sundays. Hale intervenes on Proctor's behalf, and Proctor speaks up for the upright women, particularly Rebecca, who have been condemned.

Danforth tells Proctor that his wife had said that morning that she was pregnant, and, if this is true, he would release her for a year. If Proctor's aim was to release his wife, would he now drop his charge? John looks at Giles and Francis and says he cannot because their wives are also condemned. Danforth suspends the court and looks at the deposition Proctor had brought, signed by ninety-one respected members of the community testifying to the good characters of Rebecca, Martha and Elizabeth. Parris says this is an attack on the court, but Hale asks if every defence is an attack on the court. Danforth, on Hathorne's instigation, tells Cheever to draw up warrants for the arrest of all ninety-one for examintion. Francis is horrified because he had told them all that no harm would come to them if they signed. Mary sobs and Proctor tells her no harm will come to her if she does good. Proctor also gives Danforth Giles' deposition (against Putnam) and Danforth tells Parris to fetch Putnam.

Commentary

Mary Warren, was, perhaps, the one person who could have shown that the court was 'deceived', but in such an intense atmosphere of suspicion, hatred and vindictiveness, she is too frightened and intimidated to speak out. Although she is now the central person on the stage, she says hardly anything. She does state, 'It were pretence, sir', and answers, 'Aye, sir', to Danforth's question about the other girls 'pretending', but these categorical statements are lost amongst the vindictiveness of Parris, the eagerness of Giles, the excited doubt of Hale, and the determination of Proctor to overthrow the authority of the court; although he denies, '*with the faintest faltering*', that this is his intention, there is no doubt that he wants Mary's evidence to achieve more than the release of his own wife. Proctor's tearing up the warrant, not going to church, and ploughing on Sundays, although Hale says, 'I cannot think you may judge the man on such evidence', all count against him.

But the decisive factor in this scene is the announcement that Elizabeth is pregnant, and given the opportunity to have her released for a year and drop his charge (which is that Mary 'never saw spirits'), Proctor, after glancing at Francis and Giles, refuses to do so. His simple statements: 'These are my friends. Their wives are also accused' are such a clear indication of Proctor's unselfish goodness, that Danforth is obviously impressed:

whereas previously he had said, 'I accept no depositions', he now, 'with a sudden briskness of manner', asks Proctor to present his deposition.

But even this turns to disaster, because Danforth, on the prompting of Hathorne and Parris, orders all ninety-one to be arrested for examination, and Francis knows well enough that he had brought trouble on these innocent people.

Meanwhile, Mary Warren, the one person who could have changed events, is forgotten until she 'sobs' after Danforth's words 'them that fear not light will surely praise it'. But even here, after further encouragement from Parris, she is forgotten again when the eccentric Giles wants Proctor to give Danforth his deposition, although Danforth had encouraged Proctor to continue with his evidence with the words: 'Come, man, we wait you'. And as soon as Giles begins with his eccentric anecdotes, and then his case against Putnam, Proctor's main case is completely side-tracked.

Notice that the title of the play is suggested by some words in this scene. Danforth says: 'We burn a hot fire here; it melts down all conceal-ment', and there is irony in Proctor's reply: 'I know that, sir'. He is the one who is going to be put in the crucible.

This scene gives clear evidence to differentiate the characters involved: Parris is shown as a vindictive bigot; Danforth is shown as a man who is prepared to listen, but has no doubts about 'spirits' and the righteousness of the law; Proctor's unselfish concern for others is demonstrated; Hale's confused doubts are shown; and Giles is revealed as Miller describes him, 'a crank and a nuisance, but withal a deeply innocent and brave man'.

Act 3 – to entry of Susanna, Mercy, Betty and Abigail

Summary

When Putnam enters, Danforth tells him he is accused by Corey of prompting his daughter to name George Jacobs as a witch so he can then buy his land. Giles' 'proof' is that an 'honest man' had heard Putnam say this. Giles refuses to name this man and is arrested for contempt of court, although both Hale and Proctor intervene on his behalf.

At last Mary Warren's deposition is presented, in which she swears the girls are lying. Hale tries to argue that as this 'goes to the heart of the matter', a lawyer should be employed to present the case, but Danforth refuses because the only possible witnesses in witchcraft are the witches themselves and their victims. Danforth reads the deposition, asks Cheever to call the other girls, and, before they arrive, asks Mary if Proctor had threatened her. She denies this, and when questioned, tells Danforth she had lied in court. Danforth warns her that she was either lying in court, or she is lying now. Mary says she can lie no more because she is 'with God'.

But Giles, in his anger, sees the truth that Danforth is 'only playin' you!'

Commentary

Giles' egocentricity is further revealed in this scene: he cannot see the wider issues involved, as can Proctor and Francis, but only the personal matters, and he wants to get some revenge on Putnam, whom he dislikes. But Giles' bravery and concern are shown by his refusal to name his witness.

Giles' deposition, of course, completely side-tracks the main argument of this act (Mary's evidence), but Miller purposely introduces this inter-lude to show how 'witch-hunts', at any time, in any society, are used by people to take revenge and pay old scores, so that the primary issues become confused. Hale's intervention also shows a general truth about witch-hunts: they generate such fear that people are afraid to tell the truth. But Giles, in his anger, sees the truth that Danforth is 'only playin' you!'

Proctor again tries to be the peacemaker and behave reasonably, and eventually hands Danforth the deposition. This is a dramatic moment for Hale, because he has signed 72 death warrants, and if what Mary says is true, his own crime is unthinkable. But nevertheless, he has the honesty, and bravery, to argue that the case, which 'goes to the heart of the matter', should be argued by a lawyer because the claim is 'so weighty'. From a rather comic figure, so sure of his learning with his pile of books, Hale has become, with his doubt, a figure with tragic potential.

But Danforth is blinded by his own authority and lack of doubt in his justice. He reveals that he is the one who is really bewildered – by his belief that the only possible witnesses in witchcraft are the witches and their victims, and he makes any doubting of this a questioning of his own probity. So Hale is easily defeated.

Danforth's reading of the deposition, although nothing is said, is a very dramatic moment in the play. Notice that Miller gives precise stage instruc-tions for nearly every character, which 'places' them, both for their physical actions, and for their characters. Notice the comment about Cheever, *'the sublime official'*, who does his duty in any witch-hunt, even being *'apologetic'* about it, as he was earlier when he gave evidence about Proctor ploughing on Sundays.

Then Danforth's stage direction – *'lifts his eyes, stands up, takes out a kerchief and blows his nose'* – heralds a very tense moment, a possible turning point in the whole case, so Parris's untimely intervention gets the outburst from Danforth it deserves. The dramatic action is now firmly centred on Danforth, so when, at last, he turns to Mary, the atmosphere is tense. But Mary, although threatened, speaks out honestly, if weakly, before breaking into sobs just before the other girls enter.

Act 3 – to Proctor's denunciation of Abigail as a whore

Summary
Danforth tells the four girls of Mary Warren's deposition. (Notice that Betty has recovered, and so, presumably, has Ruth.) Abigail says Mary is lying about the pretence, and also about the needle in the poppet. When asked, Abigail says Goody Proctor always kept poppets in the house. Proctor denies this, accuses Abigail of plotting to murder his wife, mentions her being put out of the meeting house for laughter, and the dancing naked in the woods. Parris has to admit to seeing the dancing.

Hathorne asks why Mary fainted in court if she had not been confronted by witchery. When Mary says it was pretence, Hathorne and Parris ask her to pretend to faint now. Mary cannot, but says she thought she saw spirits, but did not, although everybody seemed to believe in them. Danforth seems to be impressed, and asks Abigail if the spirits could have been illusion. Abigail reacts angrily to the questioning, and warns Danforth that his wits may be turned by the power of Hell.

Then Abigail suddenly, with a frightened look, clasps her arms about her, looks at Mary, and says a cold wind has come. The other girls join in, shivering and with chattering teeth. Proctor says they are pretending, but Danforth asks Mary if she is witching them. Abigail cries to Heaven to take the shadow away. Proctor pulls Abigail to her feet by her hair, and denounces her as a whore.

Commentary
Now that we have reached 'the heart of the matter', Danforth's asking the girls to sit, and then his deliberate putting of the points to them, is a deliberately slow introduction to what is rapidly going to '*grow into a nightmare*', and then a violent ending to the scene. Notice there is a '*slight pause*' between each point, and a '*pause*' at the end before he asks Abigail to rise. Abigail and Mary now confront each other across the stage, with Danforth between them, looking from one to the other. But it is an unequal battle because Mary is a weak character who does want to be 'with God', whereas Abigail is strong, with no moral compunction. She, of course, says Mary lies, even sounds '*indignant*' at being questioned, and then herself tells the deliberate lie that Goody Proctor always kept poppets in the house.

This has the desired effect of provoking Proctor, turning the attention away from Abigail and giving Parris and Hathorne the opportunity to provoke Proctor further, until Danforth has to warn him that he is charging Abigail, whom Danforth calls a 'child', with a murder plot. Proctor's '*furious*' sarcastic remark about the dragon with five legs is the beginning of his undoing. Until then, he had been '*speaking reasonably, restraining all his fears, his anger, his anxiety'*. Now it is Abigail's deliberate lie that has provoked his sense of guilt. But, rather weakly, he tries to blacken Abigail's name by mentioning the laughter at prayer, and the dancing in the woods. These accusations do not touch himself, but they only serve, once again, to take the interest away from 'the heart of the matter'. Notice that Abigail says nothing during all the following exchanges. Parris, yet again, tries to turn these accusations against Proctor, but now he is put in his place, with Hale as witness, having to admit that he saw the girls dancing. Then he tells a lie when he denies he saw them naked; this would reflect badly on himself. But the dancing makes Abigail not such a reliable witness in Danforth's eyes.

To relieve Danforth of his *'worry'*, for even he is now having doubts, Hathorne comes in with a completely new diversion, but one which enacts on the stage how the girls were 'possessed by spirits'. When Mary said she only 'pretended' to faint before, it seems only reasonable to ask her to pretend to faint again. But Mary, of course, cannot faint to order. She cannot explain why, except she has 'no *sense* of it'. This is a very dramatic scene where she tries to faint, and then tries to explain that it was a 'trick', but she 'thought' she saw spirits. But her attempted explanation is full enough to let the audience know how the girls' hysteria, which would have physical manifestations such as fainting and going cold, was self-induced by auto-suggestion. And it was assisted by so many of the older people seeming to believe in the 'spirits' too. This is Mary's strongest moment: she knows that a trick is being played against her, and she tries desperately to explain herself: 'It were only sport in the beginning, sir, but then the whole world cried spirits.'

Parris again tries to intervene because he can see that Danforth *'seems to be struck'* by Mary's story; but Danforth ignores him, and turns *'worriedly'* to Abigail to question her again. Abigail, cornered, first of all acts as if offended for being 'mistrusted, denied, questioned', and then even has the effrontery to threaten Danforth himself. But then the inspiration comes to her to put on one of her 'acts'. Mary could not 'pretend' to faint; but now Abigail shows how the 'trick' can be done, and the other girls hysterically, immediately respond. And, of course, she frightens Mary, who has been so close to exposing the girls' deception, by accusing her of witching them with the 'cold wind'.

Proctor can say, 'They're pretending', but notice that Danforth, a man of his time in spite of all his learning, is *'himself engaged and entered by Abigail'*. When Mary, *'with a hysterical cry'*, runs from Proctor, he knows he has lost his case. And when Abigail cries to her 'Heavenly Father', he can stand the hypocrisy no longer, and he reacts violently himself. Abigail has provoked him into his own destruction.

Act 3 – to end of act

Summary

Everyone is dumbfounded by Proctor's words, but Abigail denies his charge. John proves his words by admitting he had had sexual intercourse with her in his cattle shed. His wife had turned her out. Now, he says, Abigail wanted vengeance so she could claim him after his wife's death. Abigail still denies it, and threatens to leave.

Danforth tells Parris to bring Elizabeth into court, and tells Abigail and Proctor to turn their backs. When Elizabeth enters, Danforth tells her not to look at her husband, but to say why she had turned Abigail out. She admits that she thought John had fancied Abigail, but denies that John was a lecher. As John had previously told Danforth that his wife never told a lie, Danforth, in spite of Hale's pleading, says Proctor had lied. But Hale says he believed Proctor and starts accusing Abigail of falsehood.

Abigail starts looking up at the ceiling and screaming at a 'yellow bird', which she says is Mary, trying to scratch her face. The other girls gape at the ceiling, 'seeing' the bird. Proctor tries to say it is lies and they are pretending. But Danforth asks Mary why Abigail is seeing this vision. Now all the girls, '*as though hypnotized*', start repeating everything Mary says. Mary tries, hysterically, to stop them. Proctor and Hale try to tell Danforth that the girls are 'gulling', but Danforth himself has grown hysterical and accuses Mary of having a compact with the Devil. Mary tries to deny this, but when the girls run away, screaming, saying the 'bird' is swooping down, Mary screams with them, accuses Proctor of being 'the Devil's man', and rushes to Abigail. Proctor appeals to Hale, but Danforth refuses to hear him, whereon Hale denounces the proceedings. Proctor says, 'God is dead!' and Danforth tells the marshal to take him and Corey to prison.

Commentary

Although there is no stage direction to indicate it, the girls obviously stop their 'pretending' as soon as Proctor names Abigail as a whore. The 'cold wind' immediately stops blowing, which proves Proctor's point that they were pretending. But now that Abigail has provoked him into his final revelation of his own guilt, everyone is so '*dumbfounded*' or '*horrified*', that nobody notices. Although there is no stage direction, Abigail's 'Mr Danforth, he is lying' is said composedly and coldly: she has quickly regained control of herself, as Proctor points out again with 'she'll suck a scream to stab me with'. (I take it this means 'She will swallow her hysteria in order to destroy me.') Notice Francis's 'horrified' comment to John, and John's compassionate reply.

This is a great scene for dramatic acting from Proctor. Notice the stage directions carefully, although they are almost superfluous. Proctor's words speak of his *'agony'*, *'his life collapsing about him'*, *'his great shame'*, his *'being overcome'*. It is the pent-up sense of his shame and guilt of the last *'eight months'* that is being released, the betrayal of his wife's trust in him, for which she is now being charged. He now admits that he 'lusted', and by using the same word, 'promise', he acknowledges the truth of what Elizabeth had said earlier: 'There is a promise made in any bed'. And the word 'sweat' also reflects Abigail's phrase, 'sweated like a stallion', used at the beginning of the play.

Abigail is the only person on the stage not to react with horror or astonishment. After all, it is no surprise to her. But now that she is in danger of being exposed, not only as a 'whore', but also as an unreliable witness, she reacts like the brazen hussy she is, threatens to run away, and then, uses her power on Danforth, *'stepping up to him'*, so that even he *'cannot speak'*. It is only when she actually starts for the door that he orders her back. But notice, she still has *'fire in her eyes'*.

The other characters are obviously convinced of the truth of Proctor's words: 'A man will not cast away his good name.' But Danforth, the lawyer, must have evidence, and the only person who can give it is Elizabeth. This leads to another highly dramatic scene, this time with Elizabeth in the centre of the stage, unable to look at her husband, particularly as the audience is aware of the cruel irony of Danforth getting the assurance from Proctor that his wife 'never lied'. It is Elizabeth's turn to be 'in agony' as she comes close to the truth by saying 'I saw my husband somewhat turning from me', and 'I came to think he fancied her', but yet, at the crucial direct question, denying that her husband is a lecher. It is useless now for Proctor to cry out that he had confessed, because he had previously said she 'never lied'. Hale, however, at last showing his humanity, is convinced of Proctor's sincerity; but when he turns on Abigail, she immediately realises that the only way she can escape is to put on another 'trick' with a *'weird, wild, chilling cry'*. It is such a convincing act, that nearly all the characters are immediately drawn into it, and even Danforth is *'frightened'*. Only Proctor questions the existence of the 'bird', but when he turns to question Hale, Danforth silences him, and Abigail takes her 'act' further by questioning the 'bird' as if it were Mary. Abigail is about the only character who has not lost sight of the fact that Mary had been brought here to expose all the girls' evidence as 'pretence'. So now Abigail has not only to divert attention away from herself, but also to destroy Mary's credibility as a witness, and she, with the other girls taking up their cues, quickly does this by overwhelming Mary into a state of fear and hysteria. Danforth himself had previously been 'engaged and entered' by Abigail, so now the girls' hysterical mimicking of everything Mary says has a terrifying and hypnotising effect on her, and when Danforth turns on her as the source of the power over the girls, she is reduced to speechlessness until she turns from Proctor and runs to Abigail.

Notice Miller's final stage direction for Abigail, the extremely sarcastic *'out of her infinite charity reaches out and draws the sobbing Mary to her'*. She appears no more in the play, except for Parris's news of her disappearance, and Miller's final note 'Echoes Down the Corridor', where he reports the legend that she turned up later as a prostitute in Boston.

But meanwhile she wields her undoubted power over everyone, apart from Proctor and Hale. Between them, these two have the last word in the highly dramatic close to this act: Proctor in his *'wild'*, *'insane'* statements, accusing them all of guilt (which is why 'God is dead'); and Hale denouncing the proceedings, quitting the court, and slamming the door after him. But if he has denounced the court, he now has his own guilt to face – the signing of so many death warrants.

Act 4 – to entry of Danforth

Summary
The scene is a dark cell in Salem jail. It is autumn, about three months after the action in the last act. Herrick, nearly drunk, enters carrying a lantern, and wakes up Sarah Good and Tituba who are asleep on two benches. Sarah first thinks it is the Devil come to take them to Barbados. But although they identify Herrick as the marshal, when a cow lows outside, Tituba still thinks it is the Devil come to take her home. Herrick, after offering Sarah a drink from his flask, leads Tituba out, followed by Sarah, shouting that she is going to Barbados too. Hopkins, a guard, has meanwhile entered, announcing the arrival of the Deputy Governor.

Commentary
This short scene introduces an element of black comedy after the fraught dramatic scenes at the end of the last act, and before the tragedy to come. The scene also shows how two of the victims had themselves come to believe in the fantasy of the charges against them, with the irony that it is the Devil who is addressed as 'His Majesty'. It also gives Tituba the opportunity to rebuke the folks for their lack of joy by being too 'cold'. The phrase 'freeze his soul' recalls Proctor's rebuke of Elizabeth: 'Your justice would freeze beer'.

The bellowing cow, off-stage, although comically taken up by Tituba and Sarah as His Majesty the Devil come to fetch them, serves to remind the audience of the tragic disruption to the society that the witch-hunt had caused. This is developed further by Cheever in the next scene.

So although the predominant mood of this opening to the last act is comic, it has its serious undertones which reverberate into the coming scenes. Herrick's comment: 'It's the proper morning to fly into Hell' acquires more sinister meaning when it is later revealed that this is the day of execution for many of the victims.

Act 4 – to entry of Hale

Summary

Danforth and Hathorne enter, wearing greatcoats and hats, followed by Cheever. Danforth asks when Hale had arrived back in the town, and tells Herrick to fetch Parris. Hathorne warns Danforth against Hale, and also against letting Parris be with the prisoners. Cheever suggests that Parris is upset because of the contention about whom the wandering cows belong to, with all the owners in jail.

When Parris enters, he first reveals that Hale was attempting to make Rebecca, Martha and others confess; then he reveals that he had sent for Danforth to report that Abigail, with Mercy Lewis, had vanished after stealing all his money. He thought she had fled because she feared a riot in the town, as it had been said there had been in Andover. He advises Danforth to postpone the hanging of people of such good repute as Rebecca and Proctor for fear of vengeance. Only thirty of the congregation had turned up when he excommunicated Proctor. But if one could be brought to confess, then the others would be damned. Danforth refuses a postponement. Parris then admits his fear of vengeance against himself, because that night he had found a dagger by his door.

Commentary

When the grim humour of the noisy previous scene has died down, the entry of Danforth and Hathorne brings a complete contrast. Danforth's dissatisfaction is brought out by his manner and questions, particularly about the return of Hale. Hathorne's mention of Andover (where, we learn later, it was reported the court had been thrown out) doesn't please him either. When Hathorne mentions Parris' weeping, Danforth's remark, 'Perhaps he have some sorrow' is another stroke of grim humour when it is remembered that so many of Parris's flock had been hanged, or were condemned to hang – although nothing so unselfish is the cause of Parris's weeping. Cheever's remark about the cows is another touch of grim humour, although it also serves to give a telling detail about what was happening in the area when so many people were in gaol. It is symbolic of the disruption to the normal routine of the agricultural life in which the milking of cows is a permanent, regular feature.

When Parris enters he is *'gaunt'* and *'frightened'*. His aggressive contentiousness has been dampened by fear. His hurrying back to shut the door of the cell shows not only his suspicious nature, but also his fear of anyone overhearing him. His justification for leaving Hale with the prisoners in the hope that he would get Rebecca Nurse to confess (after she had refused to speak to Parris for three months!), is not so that anyone's soul would be saved, but so that all the others would then be damned.

Then the reason for his summoning Danforth so early on the morning of the executions, and for his distraction, weeping, and fear, come out. Three nights before, Abigail and Mercy Lewis, after both telling a lie to allay suspicion, had fled, possibly on a ship. And before Abigail left, she had robbed him of thirty-one pounds. It is the loss of the money, not of Abigail, that makes him weep.

But now he shows he is not as 'brainless' as Danforth thinks, by revealing why Abigail had fled. The rumour that a rebellion had overthrown the court at Andover had caused Abigail to run away for fear of a riot in Salem now that people of good repute such as Rebecca and Proctor were to be hanged. Parris's inhumanity and lack of Christian compassion is revealed by his hope that Hale will make one person confess so that, in the public eye, all the others would be damned. He pleads a postponement of the executions because there is not time to get a confession before dawn – which is now revealed as the time for the executions. Danforth refuses the postponement, but promises to try to make one person confess. But now the real reason for Parris's fear comes out. He is not afraid for any who are about to hang, or of a general riot, but for his own skin. He has *'a quavering voice'* and he *'chokes up'* when he speaks of the threat to himself implied by the dagger. His pathetic self-interest comes out in his words: 'You cannot hang this sort. There is danger for *me*.'

Act 4 – to entry of Proctor

Summary
When Hale enters, he reveals he had seen all who were to hang, apart from Proctor, who was chained in the dungeon. He asks Danforth to pardon them, and when he refuses, Hale asks for more time, which is also refused.

Danforth asks Parris if Proctor would be softened by the presence of his wife, now three months pregnant, and whom he had not seen for three months. He tells Herrick to fetch Elizabeth, and before she arrives, Hale pleads for a week's postponement of the executions for fear of a rebellion.

When Elizabeth enters, dirty, pale and gaunt, Danforth asks Hale to plead with her. She knows her husband will hang that morning. Hale tells her he has nothing to do with the court, and tries to convince her that she should persuade her husband to confess and so save his life. Elizabeth says this sounds like the Devil's argument. Danforth then tries to make her contend with her husband, but when she remains unmoved, he threatens to send her away. But before she goes, while promising nothing, she pleads to be allowed to speak to her husband.

Commentary

After having denounced the proceedings of the court, Hale has been living for three months with his guilt at having signed so many death warrants. He has good cause to be *'steeped in sorrow'* and *'exhausted'*. He is now *'more direct'* because he sees it as his only chance to salve some of his guilt by trying to save the lives of the seven who are condemned to die that morning – but he is caught in the dilemma that the only way he can save them is by getting them to confess to things they had never done. He knows this is 'the Devil's work' because he is attempting to 'counsel Christians they should belie themselves', but, when there is so much blood on his own head, he must try to save some life. His 'bright confidence' and 'great faith' have turned to opportunism and cynicism. His long speech to Elizabeth shows his lack of faith in himself, and Elizabeth is correct to call his pragmatism 'the Devil's argument'. Hale has become one of the tragic figures of the play, but, unlike Proctor, he does not become a tragic hero because he has lost all faith in himself.

However, Danforth's lack of doubt, and his resolution in the name of 'Heaven' and 'the law', are in complete contrast. He is sure that what he is doing is 'just'. But, remembering Parris's argument, he would still like one of the condemned to confess so all the others would be 'linked to Hell'. He sees Proctor, whose wife is now three months pregnant, as a possible candidate, and he is inhuman enough to be eager to use Elizabeth to plead with her husband for his life. But when Elizabeth appears, notice Miller's stage-direction about Danforth – *'uncertain how to plead, for he is unaccustomed to it'*. He asks Hale to do the dirty work for him, but when Elizabeth refuses to accede to 'the Devil's argument', Danforth tells her brutally that her husband 'will die with the sunrise', and takes her lack of tears and silence as a sign that she had delivered her soul up to Hell – when, in fact, it is proof that, in spite of all that had been inflicted on her, her moral sense, and love for her husband, had not diminished. And when she does ask to see John, she is still honest enough to say, 'I promise nothing'.

Act 4 – to end of act

Summary

Proctor, who had been tortured and chained to the wall of the dungeon, is brought in, bearded and filthy. Hale pleads for him to be left alone with his wife, and the others leave, but not before Danforth had warned Proctor that the time for his execution had almost arrived. Left alone, John and Elizabeth try to comfort each other. Elizabeth tells John that the unborn baby is growing and that their sons are well. She tells him many had confessed, but not Rebecca. She then tells him how Giles Corey had been pressed to death rather than answer the indictment; his silence meant that his land would go to his sons. Neither had Giles' wife, Martha, confessed.

John tells Elizabeth that he had thought of confessing. It would be a lie for him to die like a saint. She says she wants him living, but refuses to judge for him. She says she has nothing to forgive him for, but he should forgive himself. But whatever he does, she is sure a good man does it. She then confesses her own 'sin': that she had been 'a cold wife', and that had prompted his lechery.

Hathorne enters, saying the sun would soon be up (that is, the time for execution). Elizabeth tells John to be his own judge, asks him to forgive her, and says she had never known such goodness. Proctor says he wants his life; for him to die a saint, like Rebecca, is a fraud. Hathorne goes out shouting that Proctor will confess. Elizabeth still refuses to judge Proctor.

Hathorne re-enters with Danforth, Cheever, Parris and Hale, and they efficiently make him dictate his confession to Cheever. He confesses he had seen the Devil, but just when Danforth asks if he had bound himself to the Devil's service, Rebecca is brought in to witness his confession. When Proctor confesses he did bind himself to the Devil's service, Rebecca asks God to send mercy on him, and refuses to damn herself by confessing. But when Danforth asks if he saw Rebecca (and Martha Corey and Mary Easty) in the Devil's company, he denies it. He will speak for his own sins, but not 'spoil anyone else's name'.

Parris says it is enough that Proctor confesses, and, under protest, he signs the paper. However, he snatches it from Danforth, and will not have it nailed to the door of the church. It is enough penitence that he signed his confession before witnesses.

Danforth tells Proctor he must hand over the confession or hang. Proctor tears up the paper, and says he is now prepared to hang because he can see some goodness in himself. Elizabeth rushes to him and he kisses her. Rebecca tells them not to fear: another judgement awaits them all.

Herrick leads them out, Proctor supporting Rebecca, while Parris and Hale try, in vain, to make Elizabeth go to plead with her husband. Before the final drumroll crashes, Elizabeth says that her husband has his goodness: she could not take it from him.

Commentary

Once again, Miller uses an off-stage sound to great effect. At 'the sibilance of dragging feet on stone' all the actors 'turn', which directs the audience's attention towards the door. There is then a 'pause' before Proctor makes his last dramatic entry, 'chained', 'bearded, filthy, his eyes misty as though webs had overgrown them'. Hale is 'visibly affected', and it is he who asks for husband and wife to be left alone. Are his motives humanitarian? Or does he hope that, left alone, Elizabeth is more likely to 'contend' with her husband, make him confess, and so salve some of Hale's guilt? Danforth's blunt warning, 'I see light in the sky', and Parris's, 'God lead you now' are both prompted by a wish for a confession, so they can damn the others.

The meeting between the two, when they are alone, occasions a moving stage-direction. This is a wonderful opportunity for the actor and actress to bring out tragedy and tenderness, *'as though they stood in a spinning world'*, *'not quite real'*. The only sound, as he touches her, is *'a strange soft sound, half laughter, half amazement, . . . from his throat'*. What should be conveyed to the audience from this dramatic moment, and also the simple dialogue that follows, is the tender, loving humanity of this couple, especially when compared with the legal inhumanity of Danforth ('I should hang ten thousand that should rise up against the law!'), the spiteful self-interest of Parris, and the confused doubts of Hale. The contrast also comes out starkly when the officials, with businesslike efficiency, set about getting Proctor's confession, which he regards *'with a cold, cold horror'*.

The news that Rebecca had not confessed, and that of Giles' strange, brave death, are both threads *'to weave into his agony'*, and threads that will, in the end, give him strength. Notice that he has *'a flailing hope'* that Giles' wife, Martha, might have confessed – which would have given him some justification for confessing himself – but she had not.

Elizabeth's strength comes out in her refusal to be *'drowned in the sea that threatens her'*, and also in her refusal to make any decision for John. Her bravery also comes out in her attitude to 'forgiveness', and finally in the admission that it was her own coldness that had prompted his lechery. Although she weeps, after the entry of Hathorne, at the words, 'Forgive me, forgive me, John – I never knew such goodness in the world!', she still keeps enough control of herself to continue to tell John she cannot judge for him.

In the previous acts, the sun streaming through windows has been used as a symbol of a life-giving force indifferent to the 'madness' going on in this community. In this final scene, Hathorne's words, 'The sun is soon up', and the final stage-direction, *'the new sun is pouring in upon her face'*, are signals of death. All the act before this moment had been played out in semi-darkness, which makes this last stream of sunlight bring some glory to death.

Meanwhile, however, Proctor has gone through the agony of confessing, although he knows that much of what he says *'is insane'*. The tragic irony is that the audience do not want him to confess. It is the presence of Rebecca, brought in to witness his confession, that gives him his strength. Although, at first, *'through his teeth, his face turned from Rebecca'*, he does 'confess' to binding himself to the Devil's service, it is her calm 'Oh John - God send his mercy on you!' and her refusal to damn herself by confessing that bring out the first denial from him. But once he has found the strength to deny, that is, to speak the truth, the audience begins to know that, although he is still actually brought to sign his confession, he will not go through with it.

His final words are close to Miller's own words (see p. 10): 'Nobody wants to be a hero. . .but in every man there is something he cannot give up and still remain himself - a core, an identity, a thing that is summed up for him by the sound of his own name on his own ears. If he gives that up, he becomes a different man, not himself.' Proctor could only 'remain himself' by dying.

4 THE HISTORICAL SOURCES OF THE PLAY

4.1 MILLER'S HISTORICAL SOURCES

There are two periods of American history which provided the sources of the play: the Massachusetts Puritan colony at the end of the seventeenth century, and the McCarthy trials in the 1950s (see Section 2.7). In his Introduction to *The Collected Plays*, Miller has said: 'I had known of the Salem witch hunt for many years before 'McCarthyism' had arrived. . . When I looked into it now [that is, in the 1950s], however, it was with the contemporary situation at my back, particularly the mystery of the handing over of conscience, which seemed to me the central and informing fact of the time.' There are, however, several more parallels to be drawn between Massachusetts in 1692 and the United States in 1950.

In both societies there was seen to be a 'threat' from outside. In Massachusetts, the danger came from the wilderness. Miller says in his comments in Act 1: 'The American continent stretched endlessly west, and it was full of mystery for them. It stood, dark and threatening, over their shoulders night and day, for out of it Indian tribes marauded from time to time.' Abigail's words, 'I saw Indians smash my dear parents' heads on the pillow next to mine', are the only explicit mention in the play of this threat, although we are to understand that Proctor, when out at his farm, carries a gun for more reasons than shooting rabbits. The mention of the word 'forest' is enough, in the play, to conjure up the threatening mystery that the wilderness held. Miller says in his comments that 'the Salem folk believed that the virgin forest was the Devil's last preserve, his home base and the citadel of his final stand'. This is why Parris is so alarmed when he finds the girls dancing in the woods. In the United States, in the years after the Second World War (1939–45), the 'threat' was seen to come from the Soviet Union, which was also seen as being 'vast' and 'mysterious', and which had just proved its power by playing a major role in helping to defeat Nazi Germany.

In both societies, as well, there was an unquestioning belief in thier own rightness. The group of Puritans who settled in Massachusetts in the seventeenth century insisted on the ultimate and complete authority of the scriptures, on the necessity of uniformity and the evil of toleration, and on the responsibility and authority of magistrates in matters of religion. Many of their leaders were strongly opposed to democracy, were zealous to prevent any independence of religious views, and had no trust in the people at large. So harshness of rule, narrow-mindedness and self-satisfaction were dominant characteristics in the colony. In the United States of the post-war years, before the doubting traumas of the Vietnam War (1965-75), there was also amongst many of its citizens an unquestioning belief in the sanctity and godliness of 'the American way of life'.

This kind of unquestioning belief, and lack of toleration, led, in both societies, to paranoia about 'the enemy within'. Anybody who failed wholeheartedly to uphold the dominant beliefs of the society was seen as a threat or traitor. In McCarthy's time, these 'enemies of the state' were called 'communists' or 'fellow-travellers', although many of them had never had any dealings with communism. As Miller says in his comments in Act 1, 'In America any man who is not reactionary in his views is open to the charge of alliance with the Red hell.' In Massachusetts, people who asked questions were not identified with the Indian threat, but they were seen to be agents of the other dweller in the forest, the Devil, as Proctor was seen by Parris, his aim being to overthrow all authority.

It is because of these parallels that Arthur Miller, in his interview with Ronald Hayman, could say in 1969 that he had never written another historical play, 'because I never thought of another period that was so relevant to ours'.

4.2 MILLER'S ADAPTATIONS

Miller, however, did not set out to write a historical play, either about the Puritan period or, by inference, about the McCarthy period. The play is not concerned with history, nor, primarily, with the ideas that were current during that period; it is concerned with people, both the characters on the stage, and the men and women in the audience. Miller has said that he wants his plays to 'touch others'; and, people are not 'touched' by historical events, nor by 'ideas'. However, as Miller has said in his Introduction: 'Once an idea is "in the air" it is no longer an idea but a feeling, a sensation, an emotion, and with these the drama can deal.' So, to bring out the feelings, sensations and emotions, Miller felt free to adapt the historical record, as he states in his 'Note on the Historical Accuracy of this Play', given, in most editions, after the list of characters.

Miller's main adaptation was to make the structure of the play centre on John, Elizabeth and Abigail, although the Proctors were not major cases in the trials. Miller has said that Abigail was the prime mover to write the play: 'It was the fact that Abigail, their former servant, was their accuser, and her apparent desire to convict Elizabeth and save John, that made the play conceivable for me.' To make this dramatically effective, Miller introduced the sexual affair between Abigail and John, which created the dramatic tension between the three, and also provided the reason for John's sense of guilt. But in the records of the trials, Abigail is said to be a young girl of about twelve. So to make her the 'prime mover' in the play, Miller makes her *'a strikingly beautiful girl'* of seventeen, the kind of young woman likely to arouse the sexually frustrated John. Moreover, Miller gives her a very strong and ruthless character that derives its strength from having no moral scruples. The historical Proctor, however, who emerges from the records, was much the same man we see in the play, although there is no record of lechery. But he was a man with a 'liberated cast of mind' and 'one of the few who persisted in calling the entire business a ruse and a fake'. Little is known of the historical Elizabeth, so her character, her coldness, honesty and steadfastness, are entirely Miller's invention, created to provide motives for John's adultery, and also, some highly dramatic scenes in the play.

Another adaptation was the character of Danforth. Miller says in his 'Note' that there were several judges, but he symbolised them all in Hathorne and Danforth. The records reveal an 'absolute dedication to evil displayed by the judges', but implacable evil does not make good drama because there is no possibility of doubt and hesitation. So Miller, to make Danforth 'perceptible as a human being', creates him as a character who seems to be 'about to conceive of the truth', and who has 'a disposition to at least listen to arguments'. This change gives the possibility for dramatic tension, particularly in Act 3 when Mary is trying to say that the girls' evidence was pretence. One of the most tense scenes in the play is when Danforth reads Mary's deposition; there is, at this moment, the possibility that the whole authority of the court could be overthrown, and this is made possible by Miller's having made Danforth a person who could 'listen to arguments'. But in the records 'there is no such swerving'.

In a letter to Sheila Huftel, quoted in her book *Arthur Miller: The Burning Glass* (W. H. Allen: London, 1965), Miller says: 'Danforth was indeed dedicated to securing the statuo quo against such as Proctor. But I am equally interested in his *function* in the drama, which is that of the rule-bearer, the man who always guards the boundaries which, if you insist on breaking through them, have the power to destroy you. His "evil" is more than personal, it is nearly mythical. He does more evil than he knows how to do. . .He too, like Proctor, should come to a realisation. He must see that he has in fact practised deception, and then proceed to incorporate it in his 'good' ideology. When I say I did not make him evil enough, it is that I did not clearly demarcate the point at which he knows what he has done, and profoundly accepts it as a good thing. That alone is evil. It is a counterpart to Proctor's ultimate realization that he cannot sell himself for his life. Hale goes the other way: on seeing the deception he rejects it as evil.'

An important point to notice here is that Miller, the playwright, is concerned with his characters' *function in the drama*. (The emphasis is Miller's own.) He was not writing an historical pageant, but a play which had to be dramatically effective and emotionally moving when performed on the stage. So although he kept to the essential spirit of Salem in 1692, with, as far as the records reveal, most of the characters playing much the same roles, he felt free to adapt and change some of the details.

4.3 EFFECT ON THE STYLE

The historical setting of the play has its effect on the style in which the play is written. Here, again, Miller does not attempt to be historically accurate. As he says in his comments in the play, 'No one can really know what their lives were like'; neither can anyone know exactly how they spoke.

However, from the written records of the trials, and from other writings of the period, it is possible to get some idea of the general style of the period, and also some of the idiosyncratic expressions used by the Puritan community. Miller uses some of these to give a period flavour to his play, without making any claim that his language is authentic late-seventeenth-century. It obviously isn't. But expressions such as 'Goody' (Mrs); 'I cannot blink what I saw' (I cannot ignore what I saw); 'I'd admire to know' (I'd very much like to know); 'open with me' (tell me the truth); 'pray' (please), and many others, have both a seventeenth-century and a Puritan ring to them. There are also some grammatical uses which are different from modern usage: the verb 'to be' is often used differently; 'it were' for 'it was', and 'it be' for 'it is'; the tense of a verb is sometimes different from modern usage, such as 'she give' instead of 'she gave'; the auxiliary verb 'do' is often omitted from such expressions as 'I like not' (I don't like) and 'What say you?' (What do you say?).

Furthermore, Tituba, as a black West Indian slave, is given her own idiosyncratic form of speech: 'Devil, him be pleasure-man in Barbados, him be singin' and dancin' in Barbados. It's you folks – you riles him up round here.' Her tone and style of speech is clearly indicated by the words Miller wrote for her. But notice that some of the other characters, such as

Sarah Good, Mercy and Mary, also drop the 'g' at the end of such words as 'goin'', 'beatin'' and so on. What Miller is signalling is a form of lower-class speech for them.

Miller said in his interview in 1969 with the critic Ronald Hayman: 'I am a good mimic. I can speak in any dialect I've ever heard. It's very important to me, to know accents and the way people talk, especially in this country where speech and speech mannerisms and habits of language are so deeply connected with attitudes. . .A playwright writes with his ears.' This comes out clearly in *The Crucible*, because although Miller never heard people of the period talking, within this play he develops what can easily be believed in as a consistent seventeenth-century Puritan style, with clear differentiations between the different classes of people. Most of the characters' attitudes are revealed by the way they speak, because Miller has 'heard' them in his imagination.

But as well as the language, a certain austere tone is imposed on the play by its historical setting. This comes out in the severe Puritan costumes, and in the *'raw'*, *'solemn'*, *'forbidding'* rooms, with their sparse furniture, in which the action is played out. It is only the *'sunlight'* and Proctor's mention of 'flowers' and 'lilacs' that bring any colour into the play.

Finally, even more important than the language itself, or the tone, the Salem setting gave Miller the opportunity to use characters who were '"morally" vocal'. He said in the Introduction to *The Collected Plays*: 'The society of Salem was "morally" vocal. People then avowed principles, sought to live by them and die by them. Issues of faith, conduct, society, pervaded their private lives in a conscious way. They needed but to disapprove to act. I was drawn to this subject because the historical moment seemed to give me the poetic right to create people of higher self-awareness than the contemporary scene affords.' It is, perhaps, significant that Miller should add: 'I believe that the very moral awareness of the play and its characters who live by their principles and know very much about their own characters and situations, and who say what they know – which are historically correct – was repulsive to the audience' – that is, the audience in the time of 'McCarthyism'.

4.4 MILLER'S COMMENTS IN ACT 1

At this stage, it would be useful to go back and read through the comments on the background and characters that Miller intersperses between the dialogue in Act 1. Only a few of the characters are related to their historical originals: Parris, Putnam, Proctor, Rebecca and Francis Nurse, Hale, and Giles Corey. Even here, it is not always clear where the historical person ends and the character in the play takes over. The comments on

Proctor, for example, are partly historical and partly stage-directions, because he is described as a 'sinner', and has 'come to regard himself as a kind of fraud'. But this is the 'Proctor' of the play, and not the historical Proctor. Miller became so involved with these people, it is not surprising that he sometimes confused the real with the fictional. In an article he wrote for the *New York Times* on 8 February 1953, called 'Journey to *The Crucible*', he says: 'It will be a long time before I shall be able to shake Rebecca Nurse, John Proctor, Giles Corey and the others out of my mind. But there are strange, even weird memories that have connected themselves to this play, and these have to do with the present, and it has all got mixed up together.'

To interpolate long comments amongst the dialogue of a play is an unusual procedure for a playwright, but what Miller is attempting to do is to broaden out the background of the play, to relate the characters not only to their late-seventeenth-century Massachusetts background, and not only to his own contemporary 'McCarthy' America, but also to similar events in other times and other places.

Although *The Crucible* uses the Salem witch-hunt as its setting, and the play was conceived at the time when The Committee on Un-American Activities was beginning to touch Miller's own life, it is not 'about' either of these periods of American history. It is concerned with something much more general. As Miller says in his comments: 'Political opposition. . .is given an inhumane overlay which then justifies the abrogation of all normally applied customs of civilised intercourse. A political policy is equated with moral right, and opposition to it with diabolical malevolence. Once such an equation is effectively made, society becomes a congerie of plots and counterplots, and the main role of government changes from that of the arbiter to that of the scourge of God.' Open a newspaper on almost any day and you will find reports of 'the abrogation of all normally applied customs of civilised intercourse' in some country of the world, whether it is in the so called 'West', or 'East', or in 'The Third World'. It still goes on, because, as Miller says, 'It is still impossible for man to organise his social life without repressions, and the balance has yet to be struck between order and freedom.' And, of course, this 'repression' is not an abstraction; it is men and women, many of them innocent, suffering and dying. It is this that the play makes us feel. This is why a performance – or even a reading – can still be a moving experience to a generation for whom 'McCarthyism' is as much 'history' as the Salem witch-hunts. The play transcends its historical backgrounds.

5 THEMES

5.1 THE INDIVIDUAL CONSCIENCE

In the 'Introduction' to the *Collected Plays*, Miller shows that he is quite clear what his plays are 'about'. Most of them have a similar central theme: 'Probably the single most powerful infleunce on my way of writing [was] not only to depict why a man does what he does, or why he nearly didn't do it, but why he cannot simply walk away and say to hell with it. . . To ask this question is immediately to impose on oneself not, perhaps, a style of writing but at least a kind of dramatic construction. For I understand the symbolic meaning of a character and his career to consist of the kind of commitment he makes to life or refuses to make, the kind of challenge he accepts and the kind he can pass by. I take it that if one could know enough about a human being one could discover some conflict, some value, some challenge, however minor or major, which he cannot find it in himself to walk away from or turn his back on.' And for Miller, the humanist, the only guide to tell a man what he should or shouldn't do, is his conscience. This is true of both John and Elizabeth Proctor.

When he was writing the play at the time of 'McCarthyism', Miller says it was 'the mystery of the handing over of conscience which seemed to me the central and informing fact of the time'. However, he adds that the play 'has been produced. . ,more successfully the more time elapses from the headline "McCarthyism" which it was supposed to be 'about'. I believe that on the night of its opening, a time when the gale from the Right was blowing at its fullest fury, it inspired a part of its audience with an unsettling fear and partisanship which deflected the sight of the real and inner theme, which was the handing over of conscience to another, be it woman, the state, or a terror, and the realisation that with conscience goes the person, the soul immortal, and the "name".'

The distance in time since Miller wrote both the play and the 'Introduction' has helped to clarify 'the real and inner theme'; it has now broken out from all the accretions of 'McCarthyism', except as a recognisable historical catalyst for the conception of the play. Writing on the occasion of a later off-Broadway production of the play in 1958 (which, incidentally, had a successful run of 633 performances) Miller wrote in the *New York Times* in an article called 'Brewed in *The Crucible*' about his disappointment with the initial reception of his play, when the 'political trajectory' caused more important elements to be totally ignored. He reiterates that the play 'is examining the questions I was absorbed with before – the conflict between a man's raw deeds and his conception of himself; the question of whether conscience is in fact an organic part of the human being, and what happens when it is handed over not merely to the state or the mores of the time but to one's friend or wife. The big difference, I think, is that *The Crucible* sought to include a higher degree of consciousness than the earlier plays.'

5.2 A MAN'S NAME

Closely associated with the theme of 'conscience' is the theme of identity – the identity of the individual 'self'; in fact, until the 'self' has been established, it cannot have an individual conscience. Cheever and Herrick have no conscience because they have no individual identity; they just do what they are told to do; in Miller's words they are 'the sublime officials, dutiful'.

In an interview published in the *New York Herald Tribune* on 25 January 1953, Miller said, while discussing his new play, *The Crucible*, 'nobody wants to be a hero. You go through life giving up parts of yourself – a hope, a dream, an ambition, a belief, a liking, a piece of self-respect. But in every man there is something he cannot give up and still remain himself – a core, an identity, a thing that is summed up for him by the sound of his own name on his own ears. If he gives that up, he becomes a different man, not himself.' At the end of the play, when Proctor explains why he will not allow his confession to be published, he says, 'Tell them I confessed myself; say Proctor broke his knees and wept like a woman; say what you will, but my name cannot–'. Then, when he tried to explain, '*with a cry of his soul*', why his confession cannot be nailed upon the church: 'Because it is my name! Because I cannot have another in my life! Because I lie and sign myself to lies! Because I am not worth the dust on the feet of them that hang! How may I live without my name? I have given you my soul; leave me my name!'

It is only when he finds his 'self' which he identifies with his name, that he does what his conscience tells him he must do – tear up the confession. And when Hale says, 'Man, you will hang! You cannot!' he can reply, with '*his eyes full of tears*', 'I can. And there's your first marvel, that I can. You have made some magic now, for now I do think I see some shred of goodness in John Proctor.'

When, in June 1956, Miller, on trial before the Un-American Activities Committee, was asked to name some of the people who had been present at some Left-wing meetings he had attended, he replied: 'I am trying to and I will protect my sense of myself. I could not use the name of another person and bring trouble on him...I wouldn't make it tougher for anybody. I ask you not to ask me that question.' For not answering he was convicted for contempt of court.

5.3 CONFLICT WITH AUTHORITY

If 'conscience' is 'the single most powerful influence' on Miller's way of writing, then, for dramatic tension, the individual conscience must be in conflict with some other powerful force. In Miller's other plays this conflict comes from within the family, or from within an individual: in *The Crucible*, some of the conflict comes from within the individuals, but the main source of tension arises from individuals in conflict with 'authority'. In his comments in Act 1, Miller puts it like this:

> The Salem tragedy...developed from a paradox. It is a paradox in whose grip we still live, and there is no prospect yet that we will discover its resolution. Simply, it was this: for good purposes, even high purposes, the people of Salem developed a theocracy, a combine of state and religious power whose function was to keep the community together, and to prevent any kind of disunity that might open it to destruction by material or ideological enemies. It was forged for a necessary purpose and accomplished that purpose. But all organisation is and must be grounded on the idea of exclusion and prohibition, just as two objects cannot occupy the same space. Evidently the time came in New England when the repressions of order were heavier than seemed warranted by the dangers against which the order was organised. The witch-hunt was a perverse manifestation of the panic which set in among all classes when the balance began to turn toward greater individual freedom.

There is no doubt that we are meant to see Proctor as a man who was turning toward 'greater individual freedom'. The people he respects – Elizabeth, Rebecca, Francis, and Giles – he values for their individual qualities, not for any position in society they hold. And he finds himself in conflict with those who hold, or think they hold, some authority in the community. He tells Putnam that he cannot command Mr Parris, and adds: 'We vote by name in this society, not be acreage.' And when Parris says there is a 'faction' in the Church, which Putnam says is against 'all authority', Proctor says then he must find it and join it. And when Rebecca says he doesn't mean this, and he cannot break charity with his minister, he replies: 'I mean it solemnly, Rebecca; I like not the smell of this "authority".' Later, when Proctor says he hadn't taken his baby to be baptised because he saw 'no light of God' in Parris, Hale warns him that that is not for him to decide: 'The man's ordained, therefore the light of God is in him.' But it is just this kind of theocratic 'therefore' that men such as Proctor will not accept. He doesn't always go to church, he sometimes ploughs on Sundays, and resents that someone in authority takes account of this, because these are matters for his own choice and judgement. And he feels guilt for his adultery not because he has broken one of God's commandments, but because he has broken his trust with Elizabeth. There seems no doubt that it was the historical Proctor's 'evidently liberated cast of mind as revealed in the record' that caused Miller to make him the hero of his play. That he was 'one of the few who persisted in calling the entire business a ruse and a fake' was close to Miller's own attitude towards 'McCarthyism'.

It is inevitable, from the beginning of the play, that Proctor will find himself in deadly conflict with the 'authorities'. Such men are dangerous in any theocratic or politically authoritarian regime. And notice that Elizabeth, as well, accepts no higher authority on earth for a man's actions than his own conscience. Her final words to John are: 'Do what you will. But let none be your judge. There be no higher judge under Heaven than Proctor is!'

5.4 THE POWER OF FEAR

The power of fear to paralyse thought is another of the main themes of the play. It is, of course, associated with the theme of the individual 'self', because it takes a strong and brave character to withstand fear. This is one reason why Miller introduced Giles Corey into the play. Although he is 'the most comical hero in history', it is because he never spoke the word 'frighted' in his life that he is able to withstand the torture of being pressed to death instead of answering 'aye or nay' to his indictment. And it is the example of his courage, as related by Elizabeth, that enables John to find his.

This theme is another which arose, initially, from Miller's observations on 'McCarthyism': 'My knowledge. . .that the terror in these people was being knowingly planned and consciously engineered. . .underlies every word in *The Crucible*' (see Section 2.7).

not believing in witches is also true. But Miller conveys the non-dogmatic character of John and Elizabeth in a more subtle way. Whereas so many of the other characters state directly what they 'know' (including hearsay nonsense about girls flying over barns), both Elizabeth and John often use the words 'I think'. As the critic Dennis Welland says: 'The repetition of this formula "I think" is in fact a very skilfully-managed way of suggesting the scruples, the misgivings, and the conscientious earnestness which were all these people can bring against the diabolic impetus of the witch-hunt.' But honest doubt is no answer against people who *know*, and who also know they are *right*, morally and intellectually.

5.7 CONCLUSION

All these themes are valid for all times and all places. As Miller says, 'It is still impossible for man to organise his social life without repressions', so, in every society you will find problems of 'conscience' for people who want to keep their 'name', and they will find themselves in 'conflict with authority' during periods of crisis which bring 'fear' and 'mass hysteria', especially when the leaders of the society are sure that they 'know'. This is one reason why *The Crucible* is Arthur Miller's most performed play, all over the world, and why it always raises so much response from the audience: they readily recognise the affliction that struck the people of Salem: they can repeat Miller's own words: 'When one rises above the individual villainy displayed, one can only pity them all, just as we shall be pitied some day.'

6 TECHNICAL FEATURES

6.1 HOLDING BACK OF CLIMAX

In his 'Introduction' to the *Collected Plays*, writing about how he learned how to construct his plays to give them the greatest dramatic intensity, Miller wrote that one of the most important techniques was 'the holding back of climax until it was ready, the grasp of the rising line and the unwillingness to divert to any easy climax until the true one was ready. If there was one word to name the mood it was *Forego*. Let nothing interfere with the shape, the direction, the intention.' But, of course, to build up to a climax, certain hints, clues and suggestions must be given earlier on in the play, many of them purposely left unanswered or ambiguous so that the audience is kept wondering.

There are many examples in *The Crucible*, timed to climax within an act, or within the whole play. An example of a climax developing within an act is Elizabeth's fears at the beginning of Act 2; Mary's reporting, later in the act, that Elizabeth's name had been mentioned in court; Hale's questioning of John and Elizabeth until she denies the existence of witches; Giles' report that his wife and Rebecca Nurse had been arrested; and the climax to the act, Elizabeth being taken herself. An example of a climax spread over a longer period is the full revelation of John's relationship with Abigail: it is shown at the beginning of the play, but its full extent is left ambiguous; it is discussed further between Elizabeth and John at the beginning of Act 2; it undergoes further revelation in the dialogue between John and Mary at the end of the act; but its full force is not felt until John discloses his guilt in Act 3. (This scene will be discussed in detail in Chapter 7.) There are many more examples of the use of this technique in the play, which show how Miller used 'a mounting line of tension' and 'a gradually narrowing cone of intensifying suspense'.

the setting, so they accept the play as a piece of historical realism. But it is not realism at all: it is an artefact constructed from a special language devised by Miller and used consistently throughout the play to carry the weight of his themes, and to create dramatic tension. For example, taken in isolation, Proctor's dramatic outbursts at the climax of Acts 3 and 4 could appear to be rhetorical and forced:

> A fire, a fire is burning! I hear the boot of Lucifer, I see his filthy face! And it is my face, and yours, Danforth! For them that quail to bring men out of ignorance, as I have quailed, and as you quail now when you know in all your black hearts that this be fraud – God damns our kind especially, and we will burn, we will burn together.

But the style, with its Biblical words, rhythms and repetitions, has been so well established in previous scenes, that these speeches seem to be no more than heightened examples of the natural language of the play. But what appears to be 'natural', is, as Dennis Welland comments, 'Miller's best technical achievement in the play – his command of a new form of language adapted to its demands.

6.5 THE USE OF HYSTERIA

The historical setting gave Miller not only the opportunity for the use of a special kind of language, but also for the dramatic use of hysteria. The general hysteria that spread through the community of Salem after the first mention of witchcraft is used to induce an atmosphere of anxiety and guilt which brings out all the superstitious fears.

But far more powerful, dramatically, is the girls' hysteria when they are possessed. Using his technique of 'withheld climax', Miller first gives a small example of it at the very end of Act 1; then reports its appearance in the court at the end of Act 2; but then uses an actual demonstration on the stage with great dramatic effect at the end of Act 3. The hysterical display by Abigail and the other girls when they 'see' Mary as a great bird about to swoop down on them, and then when they repeat every word Mary says, has a terrifying hypnotic effect on Mary, and also on the audience. The action at the end of this scene is a living demonstration of the power of hysteria to 'paralyse thought'. This is one of the dramatic climaxes of the play, and it is at the heart of Miller's thesis – not given as an argument, but demonstrated on stage as a fact.

6.6 STAGE DIRECTIONS

Apart from the unusual device of interspersing long comments between the dialogue in Act 1, Miller often uses the other stage directions to give not only directions for what should be happening on the stage, when characters should enter or exit, sit or stand, etc., but also for giving comments on the situation and the characters and his attitude towards them. It seems that Miller was so involved with this play – he said he had 'never written so passionately' – that he sometimes even forgot to mention all the entrances and exits. But he is deeply concerned with his characters and their fates, and this sometimes comes out in the stage directions. For example, the last time we see Abigail, when Mary runs to her after the hysterics about the 'bird', Miller cannot resist giving the cynical comment: 'Abigail, out of her infinite charity, reaches out and draws the sobbing Mary to her'. And Cheever, in Act 3, while Danforth is reading Mary's deposition, is given this stage direction: 'Cheever waits placidly, the supreme official, dutiful'. This opens out the character, in this play, to be symbolic of all officials in all times in all places.

So this is another reason why the stage directions must be read fully and carefully, because they sometimes reveal the more universal significance of the play.

6.7 THE SETTINGS

The stage directions must also be read carefully so you can imagine the appearance of the play on the stage. The setting for each of the four acts is intended to represent a relatively small space which leads to a larger area outside the confines of the space on the stage. The audience must feel the presence of this larger space, which it does not see, because many important activities take place outside the playing area.

Act 1 takes place in 'a small upper bedroom', but the audience is soon made aware of the larger 'parlour' downstairs where many more people are imagined to be gathered, many more than come into the bedroom from time to time. The small bedroom gives a confined, closed-in effect, and the people gathered in the downstairs room represent the wider community, which Parris sees as a threat.

In Act 2, the setting is the Proctors' living-room, 'rather long', but 'low' and 'dark', once again giving a claustrophobic effect. But this time the area outside is the 'forest' and the 'farm', with 'a load of flowers on the earth' and 'lilacs' – just about the only sensuous images in the whole play: but it is from this seemingly hopeful world outside that the threat comes to the Proctors. Inside the room it is 'winter yet', symbolic of the cold relationship between John and Elizabeth. Notice, also, the 'stairway leading upstairs', the nearest we get to the Proctors' children, but enough to suggest their presence off-stage.

In Act 3 the setting is the 'vestry room' serving as the ante-room to the general court. Once again the small space is 'solemn, even forbidding', and not only directions for what should be happening on the stage, when characters should enter or exit, sit, or stand, etc. but also for giving emphasis on the dialogue and line of character, and his attitude towards them. It seems that Miller was so concerned with this play, he said he had not written so passionately, that he something even forgot to mention all the intrigue and exits, but he is deeply concerned with the characters and their fates, and this comes out in the stage directions. For example, the last time we see Abigail, when Mary runs to her after the hysterics about the devil, Miller cannot resist giving us a ghost of comfort. Act 1 of her implicit charity, reaches out and draws the sobbing Mary to her, Arts Cheever, to Act 3, wrote Danforth in reading Mary's deposition, is given this stage direction: 'Cheever waits placidly.' The sentence often, though it. This opens our the character, in this play, to be symbolic of plot, though in all those in all parts.

So this is another reason why the stage directions must be read fully and carefully, because they sometimes reveal the more subtle understanding of the play.

6.2 THE SETTINGS

The stage directions must also be read carefully to understand the appearance of the play on the stage. The setting for each of the four acts is intended to represent a relatively small stage which leads to a larger area outside the confines of the stage area, on the stage. The audience must feel the presence of this larger space, which it does not see, because many important happenings take place outside the playing areas.

Act 1 takes place in a small bedroom, and that the audience is to be made aware of the larger 'unseen' downstairs where many more people are imagined to be gathered, many more than appear, than the between time to time. The small bedroom gives a confined, closed-in effect and the people gathered in the parlour/room represent the wider community which figures as a threat.

In Act 2, 'this setting is the Proctors' living-room 'rather cosy' but bare and 'dark', often appearing a... metaphor in the real subject for this. The only stage cooking is the 'warm' and the 'warm' willing load of firewood on the door. and there... but about the only scene or images in the whole play but it is from this 'reality beyond' would denote that the threat coming to the Proctors' inside the room. It is winning symbolism of cool relationship, between John and Elizabeth. Notice also, the narrow window... apertures, the moment we get to the Proctors' children but enough to suggest their presence off stage.

In Act 2 the setting is the vestry hall, serving as the anteroom to the general court. Once again the small space is a 'known' area representing and

7 EXAMINATION OF A SPECIMEN PASSAGE

In many literature examinations you can be given a long passage from your set book for detailed study. This is not the same as the much shorter context question where you are asked to say where the words come from, who said them, what came before and after, and, perhaps, asked to give the meaning of one or two words or phrases. With the longer passage, you are usually given some guidelines, such as: 'Write a detailed critical analysis of the following passage, relating it to the themes, style and characterisation'; or 'Comment on the meaning, imagery, tone and style of the following passage.' Whatever the instructions, read them very carefully, and make sure you answer every part of the question. In the first question above, for example, the marks would probably be equally divided between the three aspects – themes, style and characterisation, so if you commented on only one of the three, you would restrict yourself to one third of the marks. This is quite justified, because you have answered only one third of the question.

Having read the instructions to the question carefully, the next thing to do is to read the whole passage carefully, not just once, but two or three times, even though you might know the passage quite well, and where it comes in the play. And, as we have seen in the scene-by-scene commentary, you must read and consider the stage directions as carefully as the words spoken by the characters.

You must try to imagine how the action would appear on the stage. Look out, too, for changes in tone and feeling. With music, changes of speed, tone, loudness, etc., are written in by the composer, so the performer knows when the piece should be fast or slow, loud or soft. Such detailed instructions are not usually given by a playwright, although, as we have seen, Miller does sometimes give full stage directions on how the actors should speak the words, and the actions they should perform. On other occasions, however, he leaves it to the imagination of the actor, or the director of the play. There are examples of both in the following passage.

Unless you are asked to do otherwise, do not spend too much time giving the plot of the play either before or after the scene. But you can, very briefly, give the context – that is where the scene occurs in the play – in one or two short sentences. In the following question, notice that you are asked to relate the passage to 'other incidents in the play'. This should be done very briefly; the main emphasis must be on the specimen passage itself. But it is one feature of *The Crucible* that certain themes, words and phrases keep recurring, and the examiners want to see that you are aware of this. Notice how this part of the question is dealt with in the answer.

Here is a typical passage that could be set, with a typical question, and an answer that does consider every aspect of the question:

Write a critical appreciation of the following scene, saying what effect it would have on the stage, and relating it, where appropriate, to the themes and other incidents in the play:

ABIGAIL: I have been hurt, Mr Danforth; I have seen my blood runnin' out! I have been near to murdered every day because I done my duty pointing out the Devil's people – and this is my reward? To be mistrusted, denied, questioned like a –

DANFORTH (*weakening*): Child, I do not mistrust you –

ABIGAIL (*in an open threat*): Let *you* beware, Mr Danforth. Think you to be so mighty that the power of Hell may not turn *your* wits? Beware of it! There is –

(*Suddenly, from an accusatory attitude, her face turns, looking into the air above – it is truly frightened.*)

DANFORTH (*apprehensively*): What is it, child?

ABIGAIL (*looking about in the air, clasping her arms about her as though cold*): I – I know not. A wind, a cold wind, has come.

(*Her eyes fall on* MARY WARREN.)

MARY WARREN (*terrified, pleading*): Abby!

MERCY LEWIS (*shivering*): Your Honour, I freeze!

PROCTOR: They're pretending!

HATHORNE (*touching* ABIGAIL'S *hand*): She is cold, Your Honour, touch her!

MERCY LEWIS (*through chattering teeth*): Mary, do you send this shadow on me?

MARY WARREN: Lord, save me!

SUSANNA WALCOTT: I freeze, I freeze!

ABIGAIL (*shivering visibly*): It is a wind, a wind!

MARY WARREN: Abby, don't do that!

DANFORTH (*himself engaged and entered by* ABIGAIL): Mary Warren, do you witch her? I say to you, do you send your spirit out?

dered by 'McCarthyism'. Mary, of course, is 'terrified' because she knows, at first hand, how such a display by the girls can lead to the victim being accused and hanged as a witch: now the routine is turned against her, which is why she utters a 'hysterical cry' and 'starts to run'. She knows the girls' power only too well, and, as she had said earlier, 'Your Honour, you seemed to believe them.'

The effect of the hysteria on the stage is to raise the dramatic tension suddenly. The action previous to this passage, with Danforth cross-examining Mary, and then Mary attempting to 'faint', had been comparatively quiet, with the other girls' screaming being reported, but not demonstrated. Now all the characters on the stage are affected, as are the audience: it is difficult for any human being not to be affected by hysteria. Although Proctor says. 'They're pretending', he, nevertheless, is also put on edge. So when, first Mary, his prime witness for exposing the fraud of the court, starts to run and have hysterics; and then Abigail, with mock religious fervour 'cries to Heaven', his nerves can stand it no longer. Previously in this act, Proctor had been 'speaking reasonably, restraining all his fears, his anger, his anxiety'. But he is now, finally, provoked by Abigail's hypocrisy, and the action on the stage reaches a sudden crescendo.

'Without warning or hesitation' he leaps at Abigail and 'grabbing her by the hair, pulls her to her feet'. Now all his anger against her, and his own sense of guilt, come out with his 'roaring voice'. The stage direction 'pulls her to her feet' implies that Abigail was either sitting or, more dramatically, kneeling. The last stage direction for her position was when she 'slowly rises' when Danforth begins to question her; and when, in this scene, she 'clasps her arms about her as though cold', she is probably still standing; but, although there is no stage direction, an astute producer would make her fall on her knees when she cries: 'Oh, Heavenly Father, take away this shadow!' This hypocritical action would make her provocation of Proctor, who knows of her 'wickedness', all the more powerful, and would explain how he 'pulls her to her feet'.

Now the centre of the action switches from Mary and Abigail to Proctor, and his repeated, 'Whore! Whore!' should resound, with his 'roaring voice' from the stage. Nearly everyone reacts violently: Danforth is 'astonished' and 'dumbfounded'; Parris and Hathorne call, 'Take your hands off her!'; and Herrick 'breaks Proctor from her'. In fact, the actions are so swift and spontaneous that Miller takes the unusual step of putting some of the dialogue into the stage directions. He wants, for a few moments, pandemonium on the stage, with nearly everyone shouting at the same time, until, 'in agony', Proctor cries out: 'It is a whore!' Notice the impersonal pronoun: his relationship with Abigail had been that of 'beasts'. Only Abigail remains calm, with her: 'Mr Danforth, he is lying!' There is no stage direction to say that the girls' hysterics had stopped, but they obviously had, and the words 'Mr Danforth' - not just the accusation, 'He is lying' - show that Abigail is trying to keep control by appearing to be unmoved and polite. Proctor's prompt comment: 'Mark her! Now she'll suck a scream to stab me with but - ' also indicates that the girls' screaming had stopped, because, although it is not entirely clear, this probably means 'she will stop her hysterics at will so she can accuse me'. His 'but - ' would probably have continued with 'but I'll prove she is lying' - or some such words.

Now, of course, John can prove his accusation, as Danforth the lawyer will want proof, only by admitting his own sin. This is why he had been 'in agony' - he knew what it would come to. He had known this since Mary, at the end of Act 2, had told him that Abigail would 'charge lechery on him', and John had replied, 'all our old pretence is ripped away'. Now, 'trembling, his life collapsing about him', the truth comes out: 'I have known her, sir, I have known her.' The little word 'sir', which he is not in the habit of using to anyone in authority, emphasises his humility now, and the repeated sentence gives his sense of collapse.

Francis's 'horrified' comment shows how the group of 'good' characters had held John in high respect, which makes his fall all the greater; and John's reply to Francis is itself humble and compassionate. Notice that Proctor is concerned for his 'good name', as he is to be at the very end of the play. But Danforth, although 'dumbfounded', still wants exact evidence: 'In - in what time? In what place?'

This gives the clue for one of the great emotional climaxes of the play, giving a fine opportunity for acting which must be moving without becoming melodramatic. The stage directions are almost superfluous; the shame and emotion come out in Proctor's words.

Some of his cynical realism comes out in his words 'In the proper place - where my beasts are bedded'. They had, he knows, behaved like animals, like the 'stallion' and 'mare', words that both had used about their relationship. His sense of guilt comes out in the admission that he had not been at peace with himself since that time, eight months before.

'He has to clamp his jaw to keep from weeping' is a very strong stage direction, and while Proctor gains control of himself, it gives a slight pause before he can continue. Then his own deep, genuine religious sense (in contrast to Abigail's) comes out in his 'God sees everything, I know it now'. The repetition of the phrases 'I beg you' and 'my wife, my dear good wife', and the speech being punctuated with frequent repetitions of the word 'sir', and lots of commas and dashes, gives the broken rhythm of his emotional upset, until he is 'overcome'. His appeal to Danforth to forgive him, and his 'turning away for a moment', gives another slight pause.

Then he cries out the final truth that Elizabeth had told him, that

totally irrational fear of nonexistent demons.

It would be nice if life were that simple.

Unhappily, the despotic threat that confronts modern society is real.

(From an anonymous review in the *New York Post*, 1 February 1953)

THE LIBERAL CONSCIENCE IN *THE CRUCIBLE*

One of the things that have been said of *The Crucible*, Arthur Miller's new play about the Salem witchcraft trials, is that we must not be misled by its obvious contemporary relevance: it is a drama of universal significance. This statement, which has usually a somewhat apologetic tone, seems to be made most often by those who do not fail to place great stress on the play's 'timelessness'. I believe it means something very different from what it appears to say, almost the contrary, in fact, and yet not quite the contrary either. It means: do not be misled by the play's historical theme into forgetting the main point, which is that 'witch trials' are always with us, and especially today; but on the other hand do not hold Mr. Miller responsible either for the inadequacies of his presentation of the Salem trials or for the many undeniable and important differences between those trials and the 'witch trials' that are going on now. It is quite true, nevertheless, that the play is, at least in one sense, of 'universal significance'. Only we must ask what this phrase has come to mean, and whether the quality it denotes is a virtue.

(From an article by Robert Warshow, 'The Immediate Experience', which first appeared in *Commentary*, March 1953)

Dramatically absorbing in itself, *The Crucible* may be viewed as a transitional piece if we consider it in the context of Miller's later development. Using a historical subject, the play shows how a materialistically instigated social trauma may fester into a sadistic fever to which an entire community succumbs. It leads it to superstitious hysteria and to the abandonment of all moral scruples and intelligence. (A similar theme stimulated Miller to undertake the adaptation of Ibsen's *An Enemy of the People*.) The fear and frenzy of the McCarthy era is plainly the fire which ignited *The Crucible*. 'Is the accuser always holy?' is its key line. But there is something more to the play than 'propaganda'.

It contains two features which time and further experience magnified. One of them has to do with marital relationships. There is a certain Puritan coldness in Elizabeth, *The Crucible*'s heroine. She forgets nothing, and forgiveness comes hard to her. Her husband, Proctor, admonishes, 'Learn charity, woman.' Perhaps it is this forbidding quality in her which has betrayed him into a momentary adultery. It is a fall from grace in his eyes. Despite his plea for compassion, he finds it difficult to forgive himself. 'The magistrate sits in your heart that judges you,' she says. 'I never thought you but a good man, only somewhat bewildered.' She is right, and the web of their intimate struggle with each other anticipates some of the marital complexities in the thematic material of *After the Fall*.

(From the editor's 'Introduction' to *The Portable Arthur Miller*, ed. Harold Clurman, Penguin Books, 1977)

It is a play in which private feuding erupts into controversies that overwhelm an entire community. This view supports Miller's idea that the problems of a single man are not sufficient to 'contain the truth of the human situation'. Yet, a play must focus upon individuals whose discoveries and decisions determine both its actions and its theme. In this instance the object of the dramatist is to show the whole man – therefore, man as individual in conflict with himself (tragic possibilities) and the society (melodramatic possibilities). The initial situation of the play is well devised to prevent the social forces that in Act Two provide the major conflict for Proctor as he becomes aware of the court and reveals his temper, his strengths, and his failings. It would appear in Act Two that evil may win over a typically blind justice. Neither a Job nor a Lear, Proctor is a prideful and strong man who, in folly, both causes and curses his fate. As in any effective melodrama, the relentless forces of evil must appear inevitable. For this play these forces involve the theocratic processes run amok. That balance that once existed between order and freedom in that society – illustrated in the play by the character of Proctor as revealed in Act One – is being destroyed. Both social and personal conflicts are dramatized in the destruction of a man by deadly fraud and by a self-imposed hypnotism on the part of a society in panic. Symbolically, the climax suggests the end of an era, the waste of human lives, and the confused state of man as either a tragic figure whose personal disaster shatters the balance of the world or as a melodramatic hero whose committed choice for personal sacrifice and death returns order to the world.

(From an essay by Walter J. Meserve printed for the first time in *Arthur Miller: New Perspectives*, ed. Robert A. Martin, Prentice-Hall: New Jersey, 1982)

FURTHER READING

Other plays by Arthur Miller

All My Sons	1947
Death of a Salesman	1949
A Memory of Two Mondays	1955
A View from the Bridge	1955
The Misfits ('neither novel, play, nor screenplay')	1957
After the Fall	1964
Incident at Vichy	1964
The Price	1968
The Creation of the World and Other Business	1972
Playing for Time (Screenplay)	1980
The American Clock	1982
The Archbishop's Ceiling	1984
Two Way Mirror (a double-bill of *Elegy for a Lady* and *Some Kind of Love Story*)	1984

The first four plays are in *Collected Plays*, vol. I (Secker & Warburg: London, 1974); the next six are in *Arthur Miller's Collected Plays*, vol.II (Secker & Warburg: London, 1983). Most of them are in separate, paperback editions. The last three plays are published by Methuen, London. There is also an adaptation first produced in 1950, of Ibsen's *An Enemy of the People*.

Criticism

Arthur Miller, 'Introduction' to *Collected Plays*, vol I. The best source of information on Miller's plays. It is, in itself, a fine and spirited piece of creative writing, and is essential reading for any serious student.

Robert A. Martin (ed.), *The Theatre Essays of Arthur Miller* (Penguin Books: Harmondsworth, 1978). Miller's own comments, taken from essays, articles, speeches and interviews, on productions of his plays, and on his attitude to drama. There are two pieces specifically on *The Crucible*.

Robert A. Martin (ed.), *Arthur Miller: New Perspectives* (Prentice-Hall: New Jersey, 1982). A collection of essays, many published for the first time, giving more recent assessments of Miller's plays. Only one is specifically on *The Crucible*, but many other essays refer to it at length.

Gerald Weales (ed.), *Arthur Miller: The Crucible: Text and Criticism* (Penguin Books: Harmondsworth, 1977).

Robert W. Corrigan (ed.), *Arthur Miller: A Collection of Critical Essays* (Prentice-Hall: New Jersey, 1969).

Biography and Criticism

Neil Carson, *Arthur Miller* (Macmillan, 1982).

Ronald Hayman, *Arthur Miller* (Heinemann, 1970). This contains an interview with Miller about his plays.

Sheila Huftel, *Arthur Miller: The Burning Glass* (W. H. Allen, 1965).

Benjamin Nelson, *Arthur Miller, Portrait of a Playwright* (Peter Owen, 1970).

Dennis Welland, *Miller the Playwright* (Methuen, revised edition 1983).

...and on his attitude to dying. There are two plays, notably on
Fire Island.

Robert A. Martin (ed.) *Arthur Miller, New Perspectives* (Prentice-Hall,
New Jersey, 1982.) A collection of essays, many published for the
first time, giving more recent assessments of Miller's plays. Only one
essay specifically on *The Crucible*, but many other essays refer to it of
course.

Gerald Weales (ed.) *Arthur Miller, The Crucible: Text and Criticism*
(Penguin Books, Harmondsworth, 1977)

Robert W. Corrigan (ed.) *Arthur Miller: A Collection of Critical Essays*
(Prentice-Hall, New Jersey, 1969).

Biography and Criticism

Neil Carson, *Arthur Miller* (Macmillan, 1982)

Ronald Hayman, *Arthur Miller* (Heinemann, 1970). ... contains an interview with Miller about his plays

Sheila Huftel, *Arthur Miller: The Burning Glass* (W. H. Allen, 1965).

Benjamin Nelson, *Arthur Miller: Portrait of a Playwright* (Peter Owen,
1970).

Dennis Welland, *Miller the Playwright* (Methuen, revised edition 1983).

MILTON: PARADISE LOST
A. E. Dyson and Julian Lovelock

POETRY OF THE FIRST WORLD WAR
Dominic Hibberd

ALEXANDER POPE: THE RAPE OF THE LOCK
John Dixon Hunt

SHELLEY: SHORTER POEMS & LYRICS
Patrick Swinden

SPENSER: THE FAERIE QUEEN
Peter Bayley

TENNYSON: IN MEMORIAM
John Dixon Hunt

THIRTIES POETS: 'THE AUDEN GROUP'
Ronald Carter

WORDSWORTH: LYRICAL BALLADS
A. R. Jones and W. Tydeman

WORDSWORTH: THE PRELUDE
W. J. Harvey and R. Gravil

W. B. YEATS: POEMS 1919–1935
E. Cullingford

W. B. YEATS: LAST POEMS
Jon Stallworthy

THE NOVEL AND PROSE

JANE AUSTEN: EMMA
David Lodge

JANE AUSTEN: NORTHANGER ABBEY AND PERSUASION
B. C. Southam

JANE AUSTEN: SENSE AND SENSIBILITY, PRIDE AND PREJUDICE AND MANSFIELD PARK
B. C. Southam

CHARLOTTE BRONTË: JANE EYRE AND VILLETTE
Miriam Allott

EMILY BRONTË: WUTHERING HEIGHTS
Miriam Allott

BUNYAN: THE PILGRIM'S PROGRESS
R. Sharrock

CONRAD: HEART OF DARKNESS, NOSTROMO AND UNDER WESTERN EYES
C. B. Cox

CONRAD: THE SECRET AGENT
Ian Watt

CHARLES DICKENS: BLEAK HOUSE
A. E. Dyson

CHARLES DICKENS: DOMBEY AND SON AND LITTLE DORRITT
Alan Shelston

CHARLES DICKENS: HARD TIMES, GREAT EXPECTATIONS AND OUR MUTUAL FRIEND
N. Page

GEORGE ELIOT: MIDDLEMARCH
Patrick Swinden

GEORGE ELIOT: THE MILL ON THE FLOSS AND SILAS MARNER
R. P. Draper

HENRY FIELDING: TOM JONES
Neil Compton

E. M. FORSTER: A PASSAGE TO INDIA
Malcolm Bradbury

HARDY: THE TRAGIC NOVELS
R. P. Draper

HENRY JAMES: WASHINGTON SQUARE AND THE PORTRAIT OF A LADY
Alan Shelston

JAMES JOYCE: DUBLINERS AND A PORTRAIT OF THE ARTIST AS A YOUNG MAN
Morris Beja

D. H. LAWRENCE: THE RAINBOW AND WOMEN IN LOVE
Colin Clarke

D. H. LAWRENCE: SONS AND LOVERS
Gamini Salgado

SWIFT: GULLIVER'S TRAVELS
Richard Gravil

THACKERAY: VANITY FAIR
Arthur Pollard

TROLLOPE: THE BARSETSHIRE
NOVELS
T. Bareham

VIRGINIA WOOLF: TO THE
LIGHTHOUSE
Morris Beja

DRAMA

CONGREVE: COMEDIES
Patrick Lyons

T. S. ELIOT: PLAYS
Arnold P. Hinchliffe

JONSON: EVERY MAN IN HIS
HUMOUR AND THE ALCHEMIST
R. V. Holdsworth

JONSON: VOLPONE
J. A. Barish

MARLOWE: DR FAUSTUS
John Jump

MARLOWE: TAMBURLAINE,
EDWARD II AND THE JEW OF
MALTA
John Russell Brown

MEDIEVAL ENGLISH DRAMA
Peter Happé

O'CASEY: JUNO AND THE
PAYCOCK, THE PLOUGH AND THE
STARS AND THE SHADOW OF A
GUNMAN
R. Ayling

JOHN OSBORNE: LOOK BACK IN
ANGER
John Russell Taylor

WEBSTER: THE WHITE DEVIL AND
THE DUCHESS OF MALFI
R. V. Holdsworth

WILDE: COMEDIES
W. Tydeman

SHAKESPEARE

SHAKESPEARE: ANTONY AND
CLEOPATRA
John Russell Brown

SHAKESPEARE: CORIOLANUS
B. A. Brockman

SHAKESPEARE: HAMLET
John Jump

SHAKESPEARE: HENRY IV PARTS
I AND II
G. K. Hunter

SHAKESPEARE: HENRY V
Michael Quinn

SHAKESPEARE: JULIUS CAESAR
Peter Ure

SHAKESPEARE: KING LEAR
Frank Kermode

SHAKESPEARE: MACBETH
John Wain

SHAKESPEARE: MEASURE FOR
MEASURE
G. K. Stead

SHAKESPEARE: THE MERCHANT
OF VENICE
John Wilders

SHAKESPEARE: A MIDSUMMER
NIGHT'S DREAM
A. W. Price

SHAKESPEARE: MUCH ADO
ABOUT NOTHING AND AS YOU
LIKE IT
John Russell Brown

SHAKESPEARE: OTHELLO
John Wain

SHAKESPEARE: RICHARD II
N. Brooke

SHAKESPEARE: THE SONNETS
Peter Jones

SHAKESPEARE: THE TEMPEST
D. J. Palmer

SHAKESPEARE: TROILUS AND
CRESSIDA
Priscilla Martin

SHAKESPEARE: TWELFTH NIGHT
D. J. Palmer

SHAKESPEARE: THE WINTER'S
TALE
Kenneth Muir